KT-362-735

IN MY DAY

IRELAND THEN AND NOW

ROB STEARS

HACHETTE
BOOKS
IRELAND

First published in 2017 by Hachette Books Ireland
Copyright © Rob Stears, 2017

A CIP catalogue record for this title is available from the British
Library.

ISBN 978 1 47367 351 9

Typesetting by Bookends Publishing Servies, Dublin.
Printed and bound in Great Britain by Clays , St Ives plc.

Hachette Books Ireland's policy is to use papers that are natural,
renewable and recyclable and made from wood grown in sustainable
forests. The logging and manufacturing processes are expected to
conform to the environmental regulations of the country of origin.

Hachette Books Ireland
8 Castlecourt Centre, Castleknock, Dublin 15, Ireland

A division of Hachette UK Ltd
Carmelite House, Victoria Embankment, London EC4Y 0DZ

www.hachettebooksireland.ie

CONTENTS

FOR LAURA AND ALAN

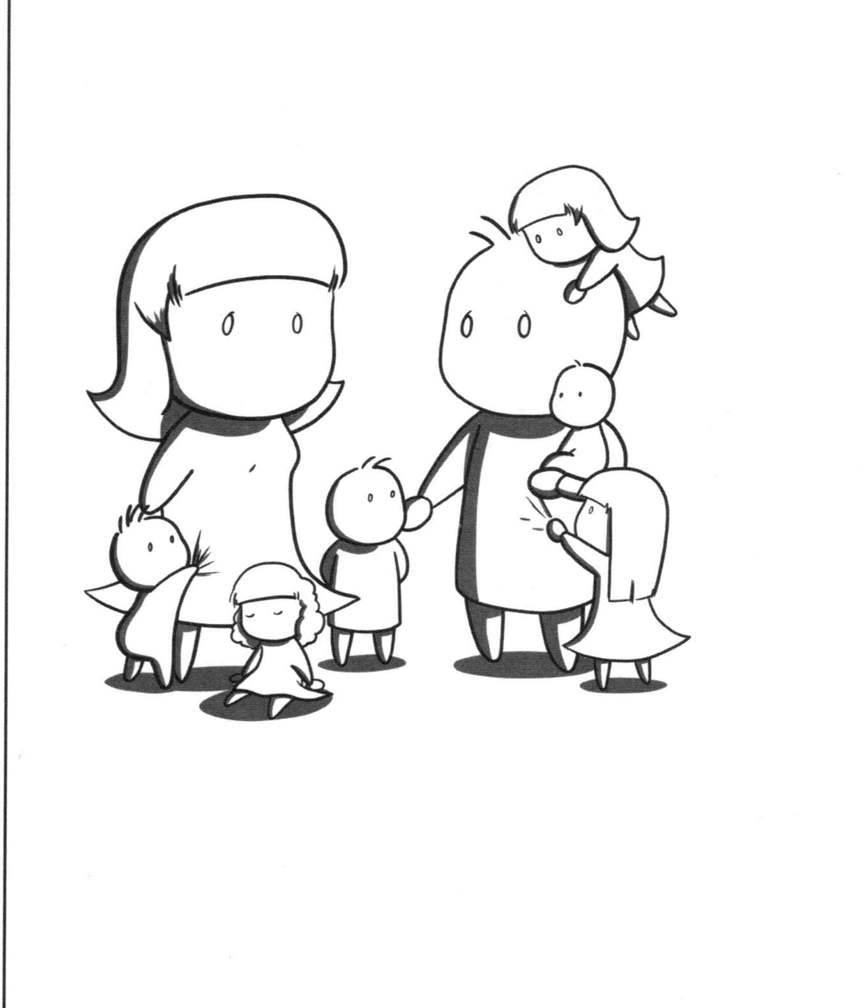

FAMILY AND RELATIONSHIPS

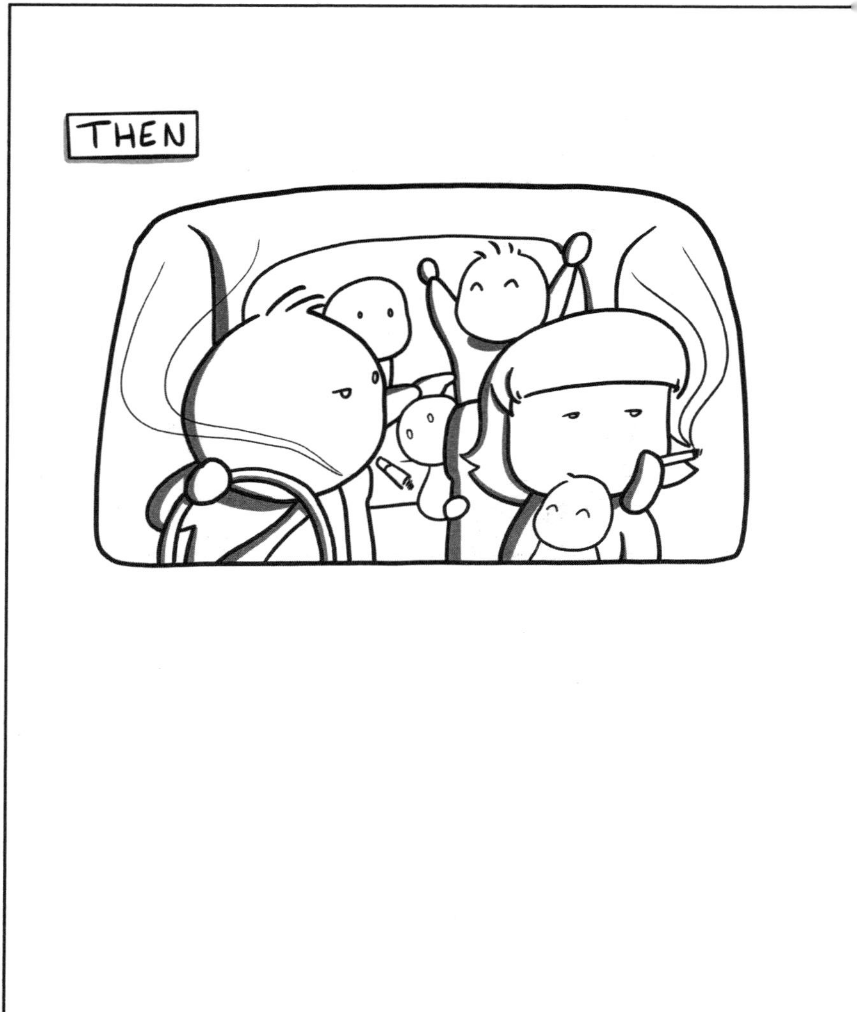
THEN

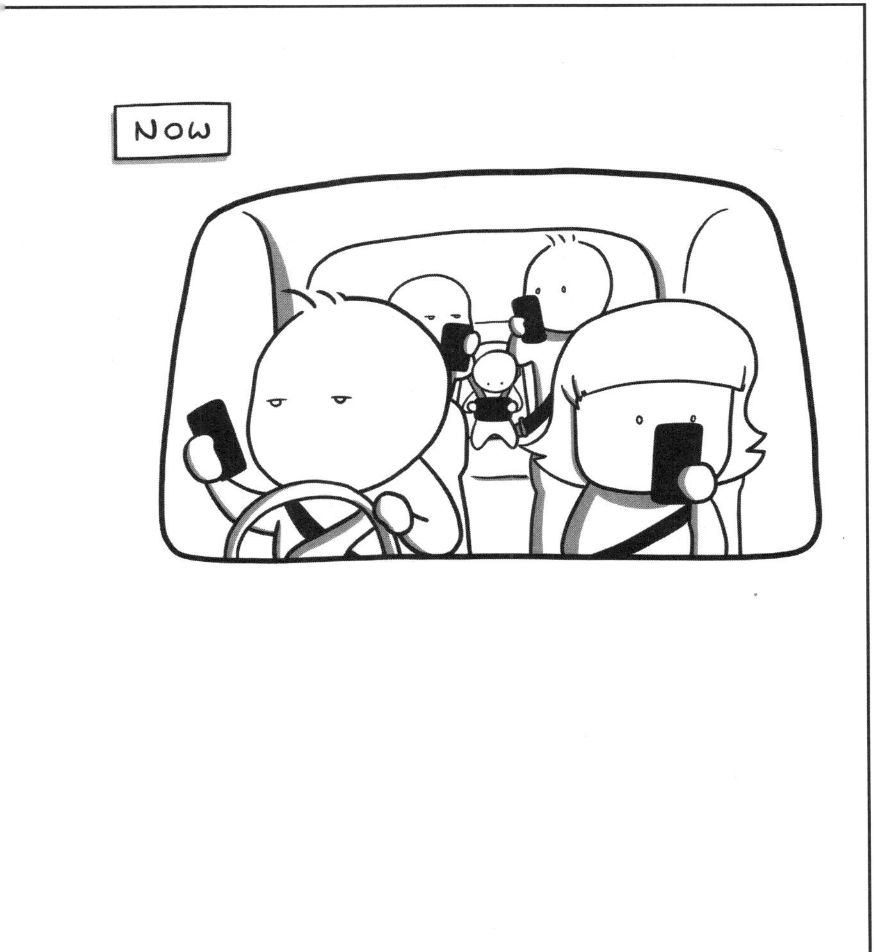
NOW

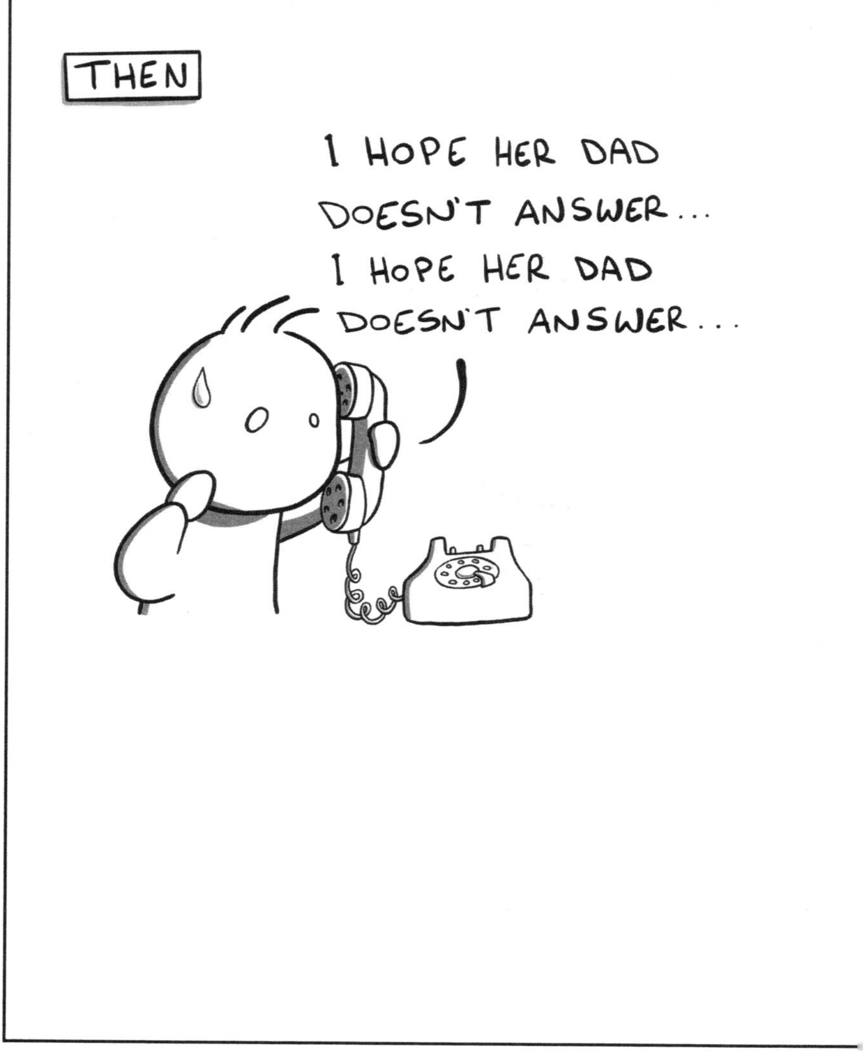
THEN
I HOPE HER DAD DOESN'T ANSWER...
I HOPE HER DAD DOESN'T ANSWER...

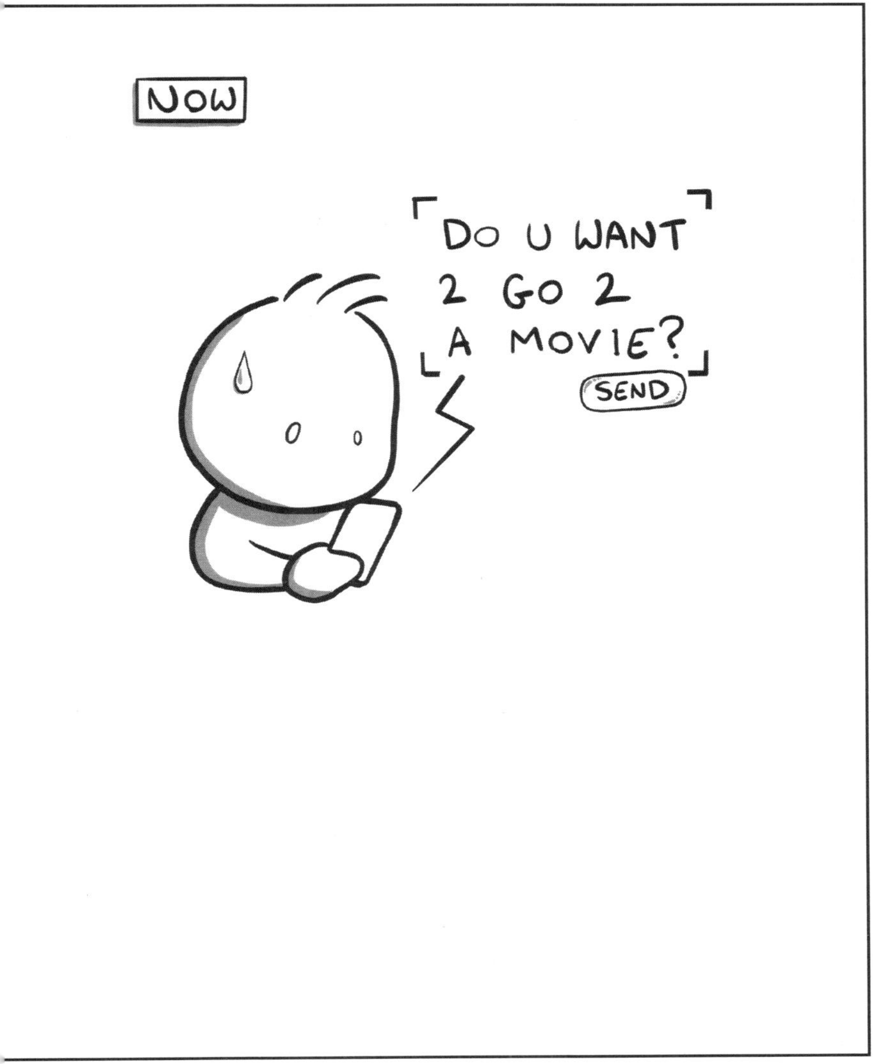
NOW
DO U WANT 2 GO 2 A MOVIE?
SEND

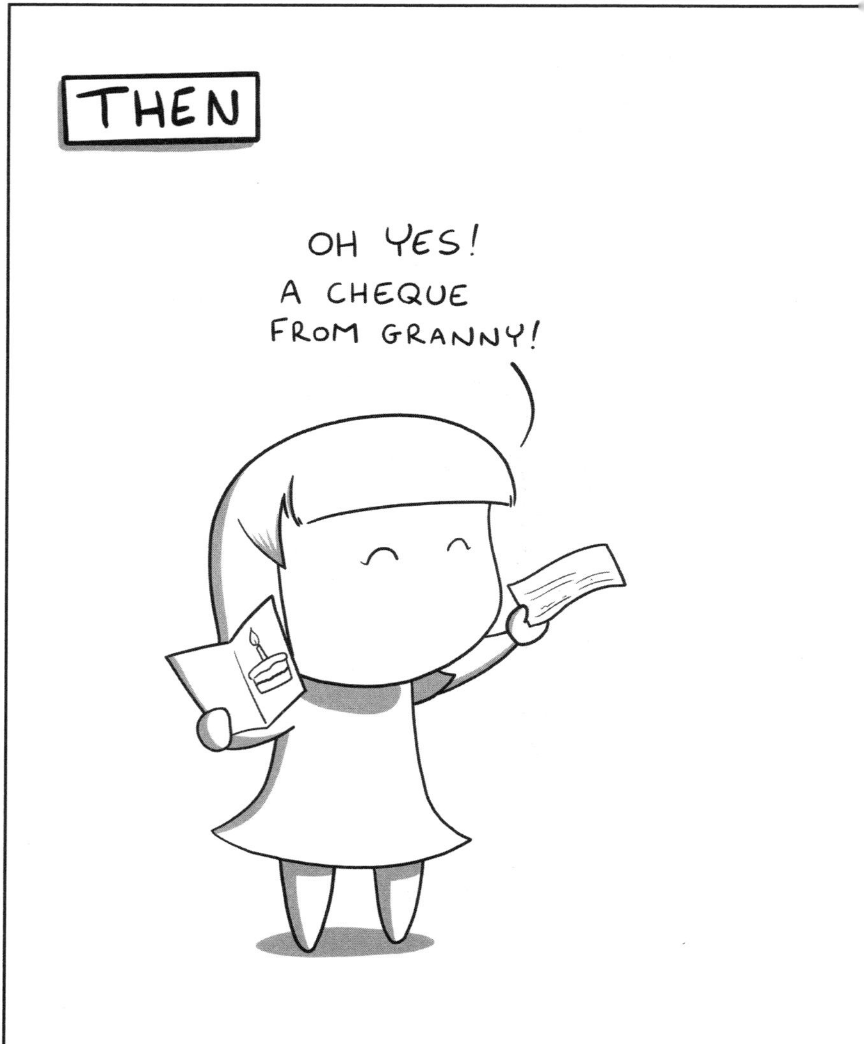
THEN
OH YES!
A CHEQUE
FROM GRANNY!

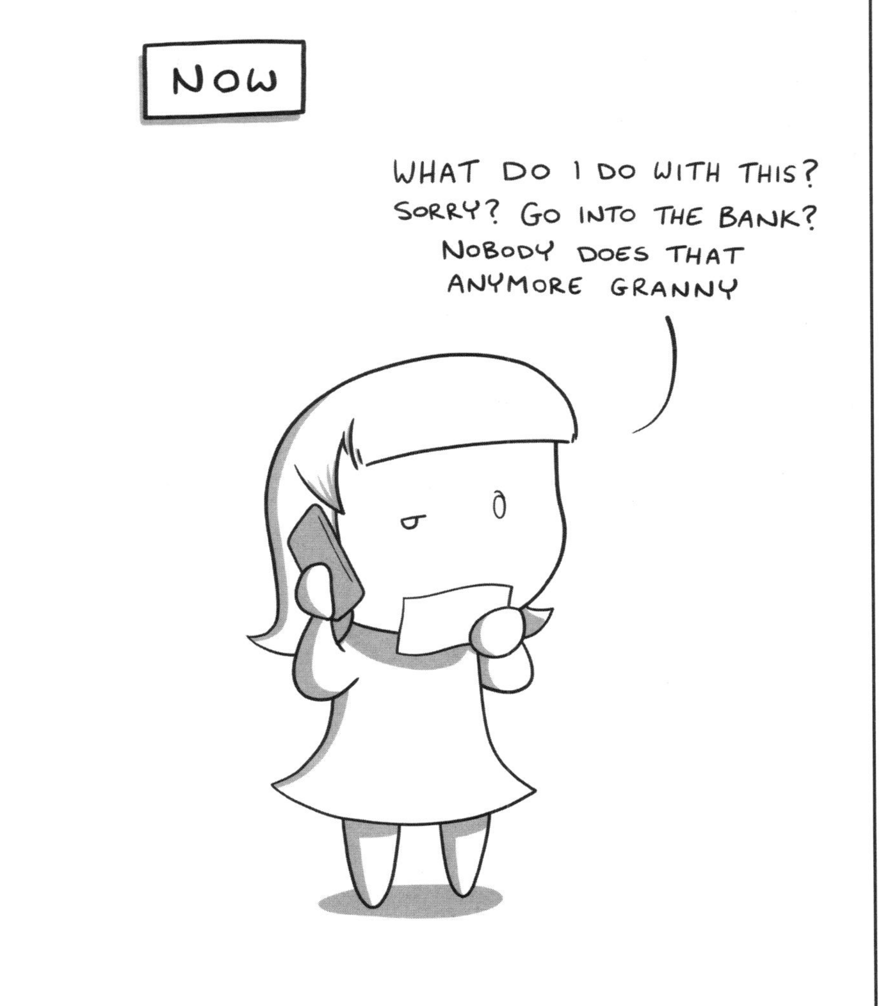
NOW
WHAT DO I DO WITH THIS? SORRY? GO INTO THE BANK? NOBODY DOES THAT ANYMORE GRANNY

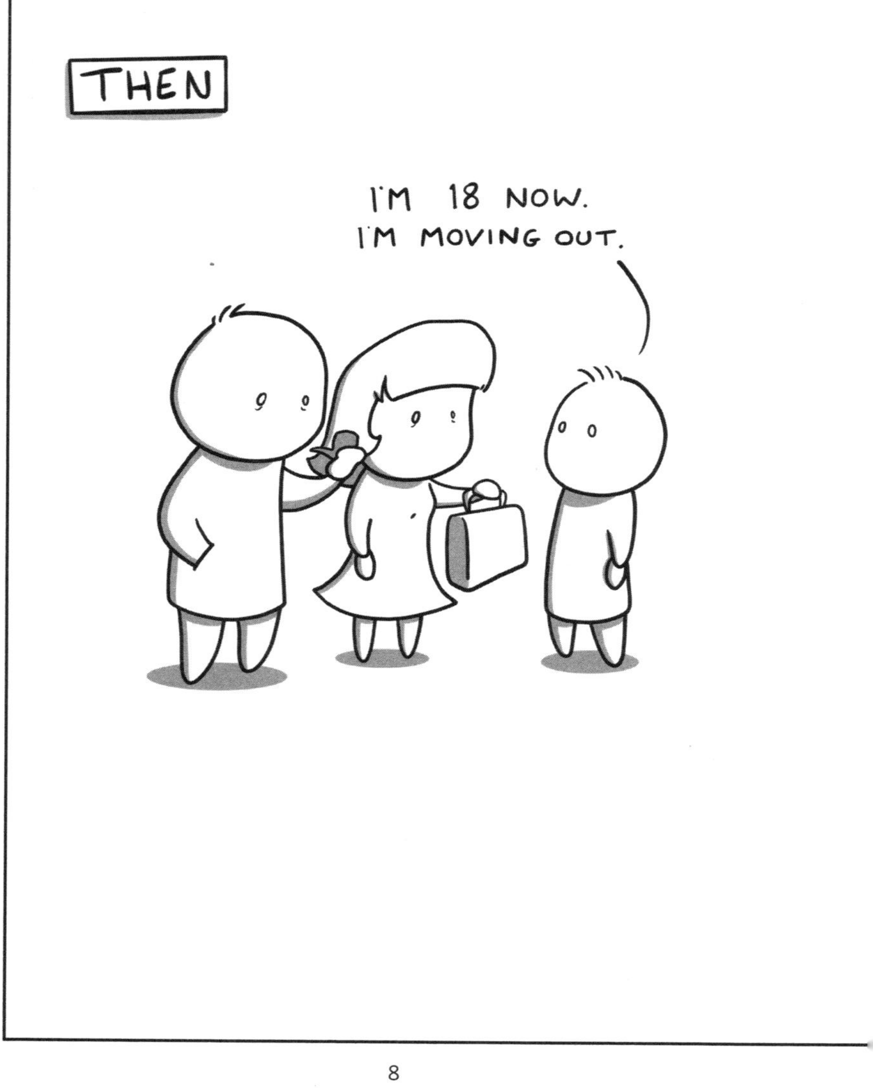
THEN
I'M 18 NOW.
I'M MOVING OUT.

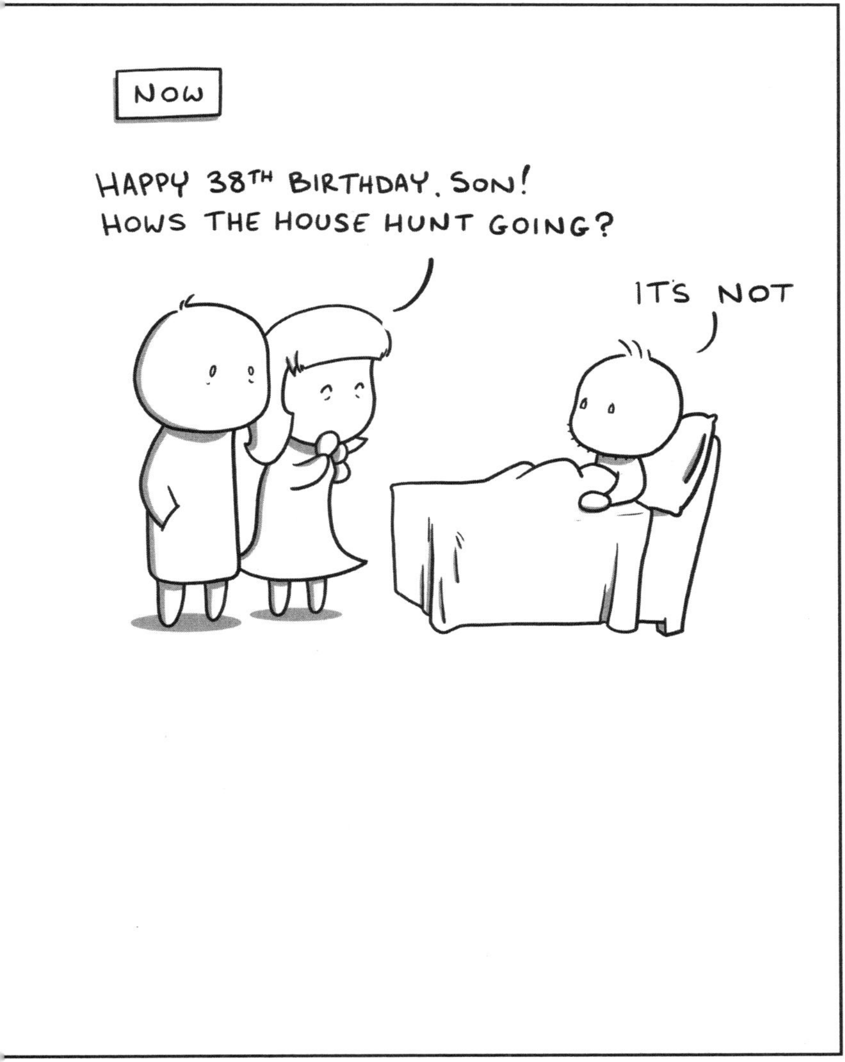
NOW
HAPPY 38TH BIRTHDAY, SON! HOWS THE HOUSE HUNT GOING?
IT'S NOT

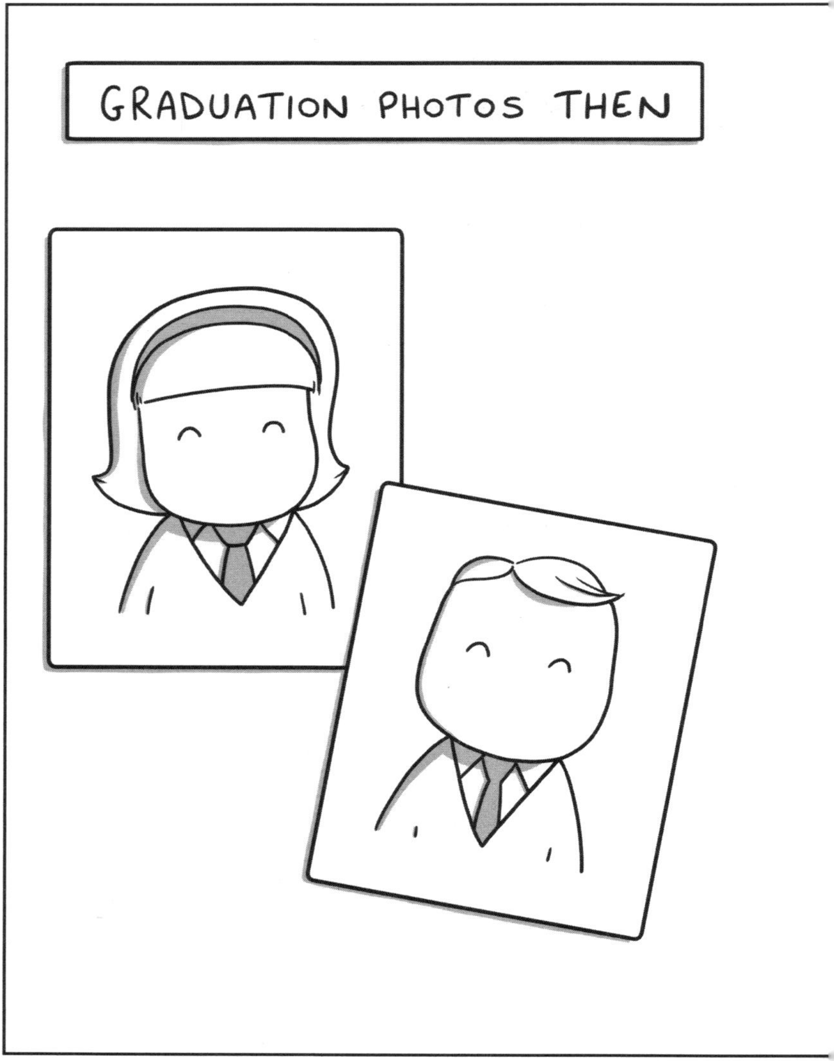
GRADUATION PHOTOS THEN

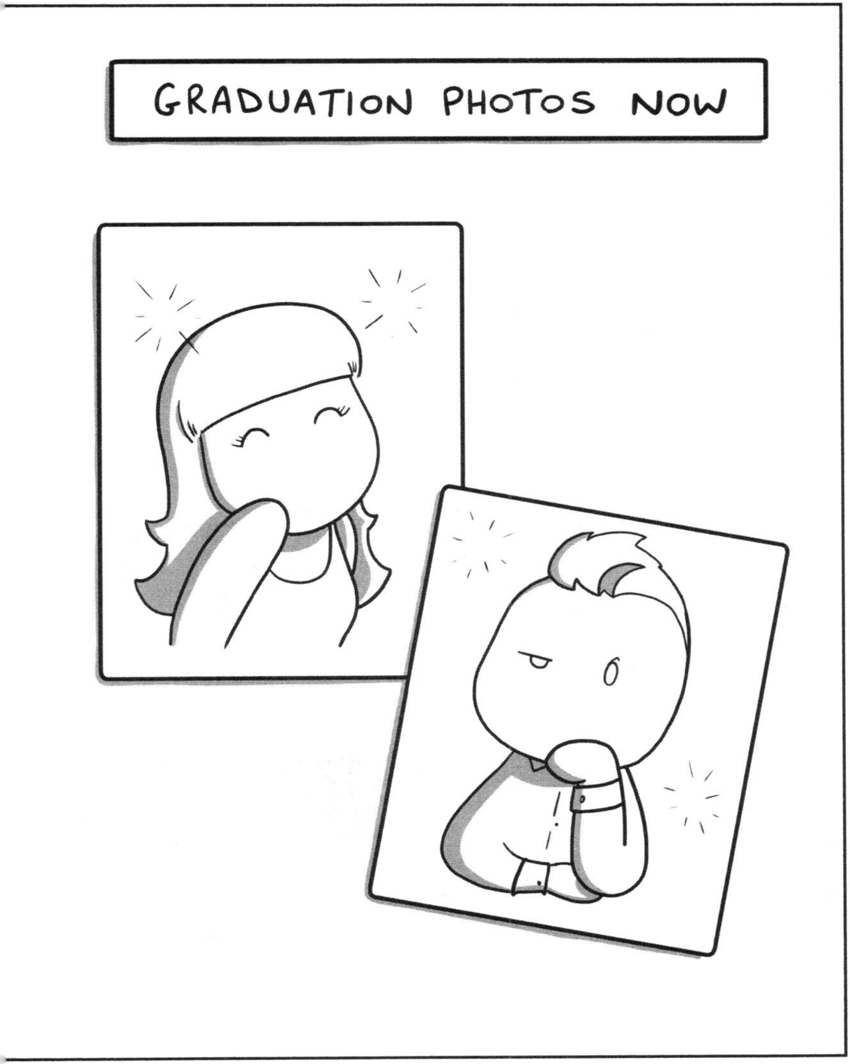
GRADUATION PHOTOS NOW

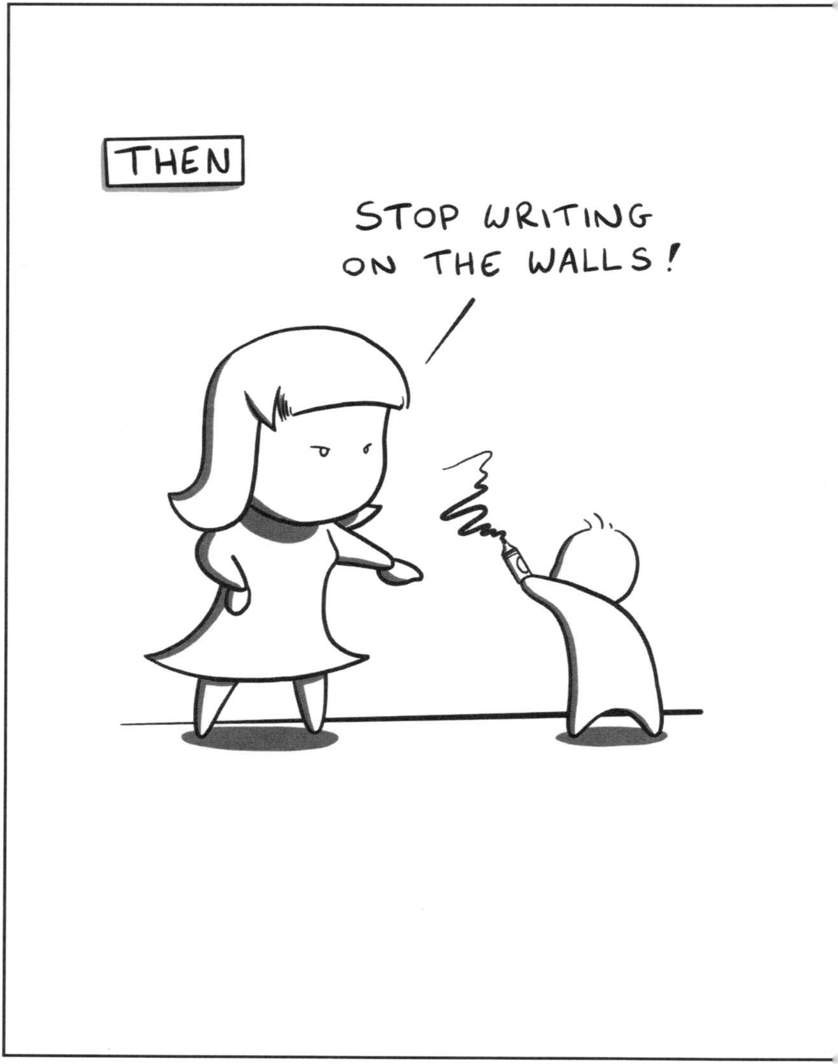
THEN
STOP WRITING ON THE WALLS!

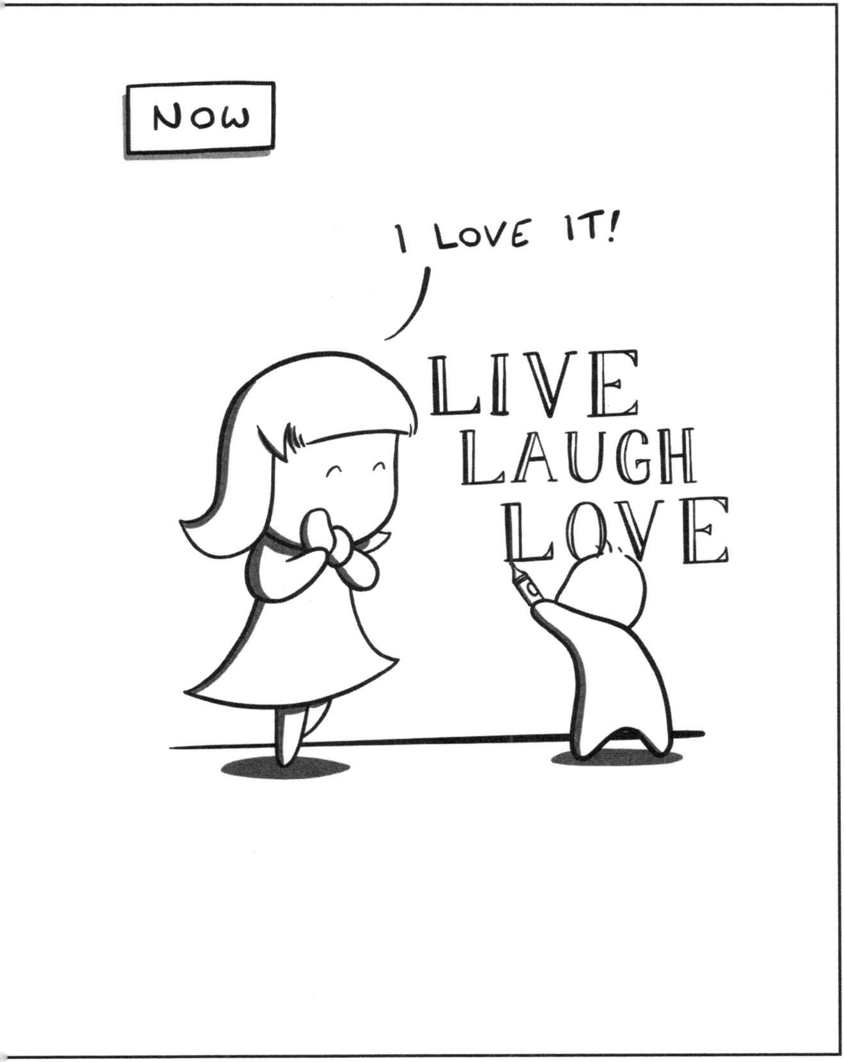
NOW
I LOVE IT!
LIVE
LAUGH
LOVE

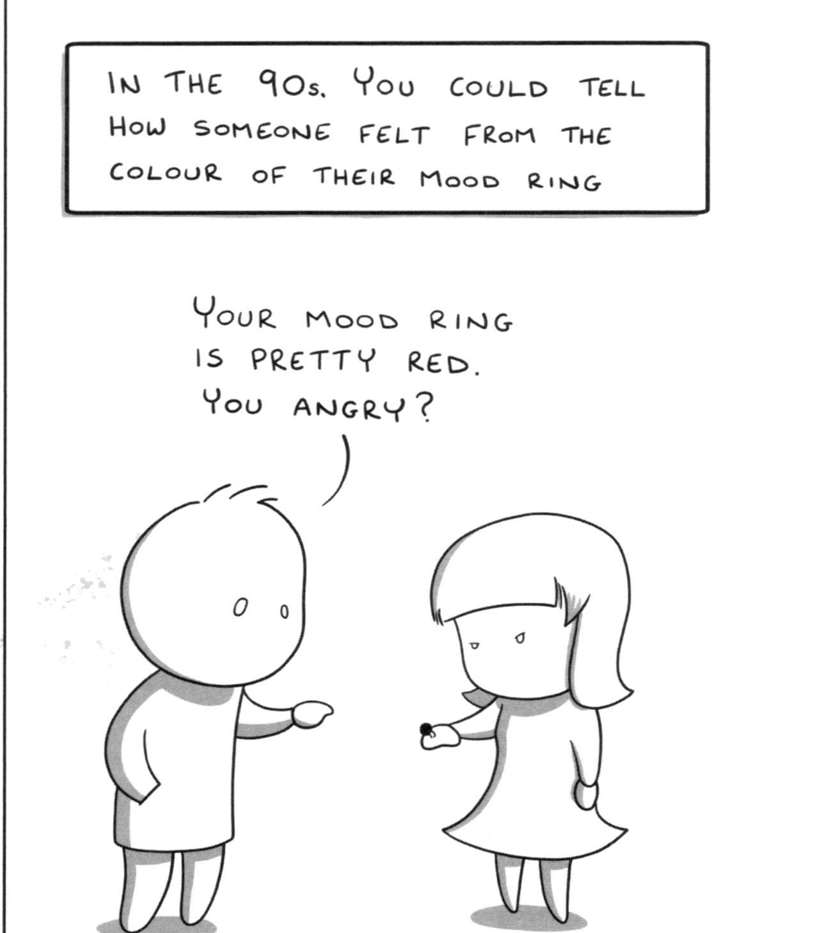
IN THE 90s. YOU COULD TELL HOW SOMEONE FELT FROM THE COLOUR OF THEIR MOOD RING
YOUR MOOD RING IS PRETTY RED. YOU ANGRY?

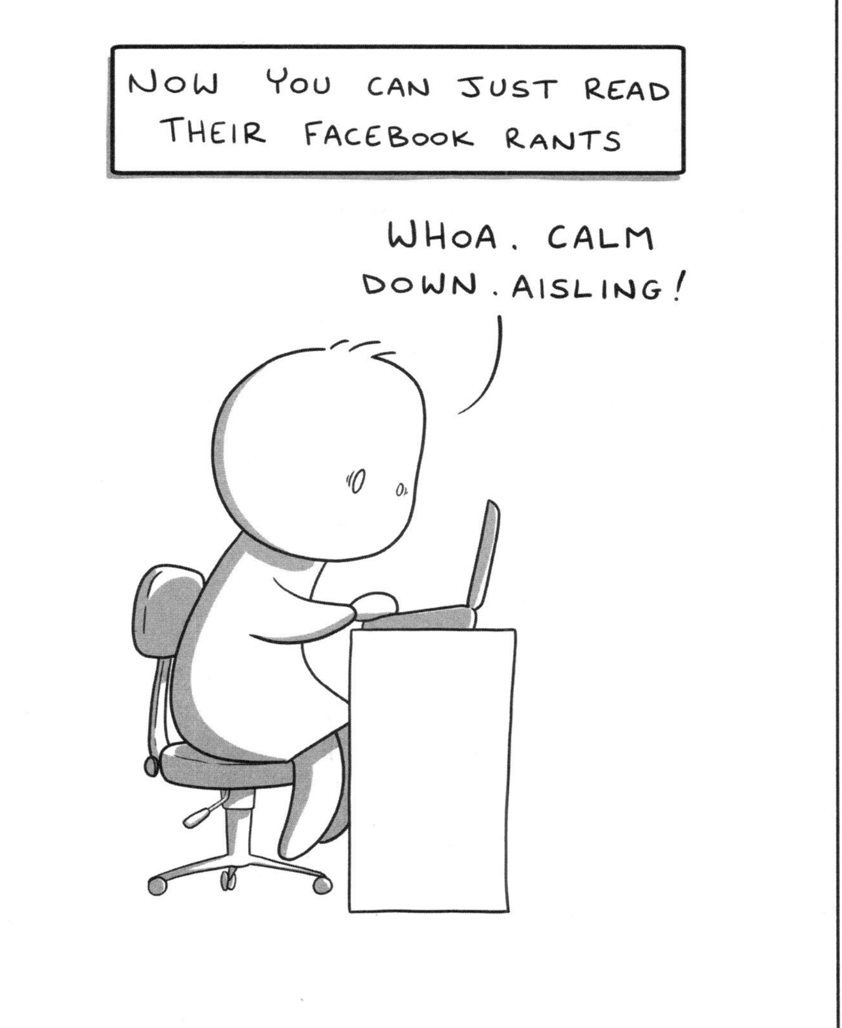
NOW YOU CAN JUST READ THEIR FACEBOOK RANTS
WHOA. CALM DOWN. AISLING!

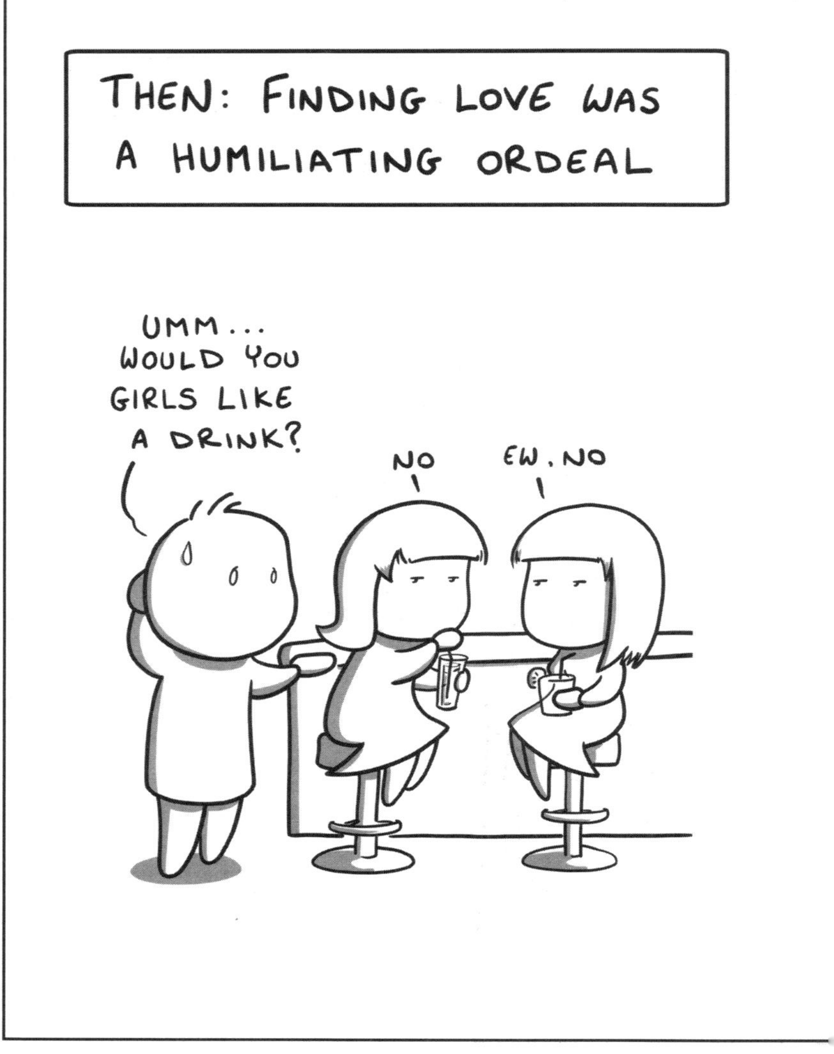
THEN: FINDING LOVE WAS A HUMILIATING ORDEAL
UMM... WOULD YOU GIRLS LIKE A DRINK?
NO
EW, NO

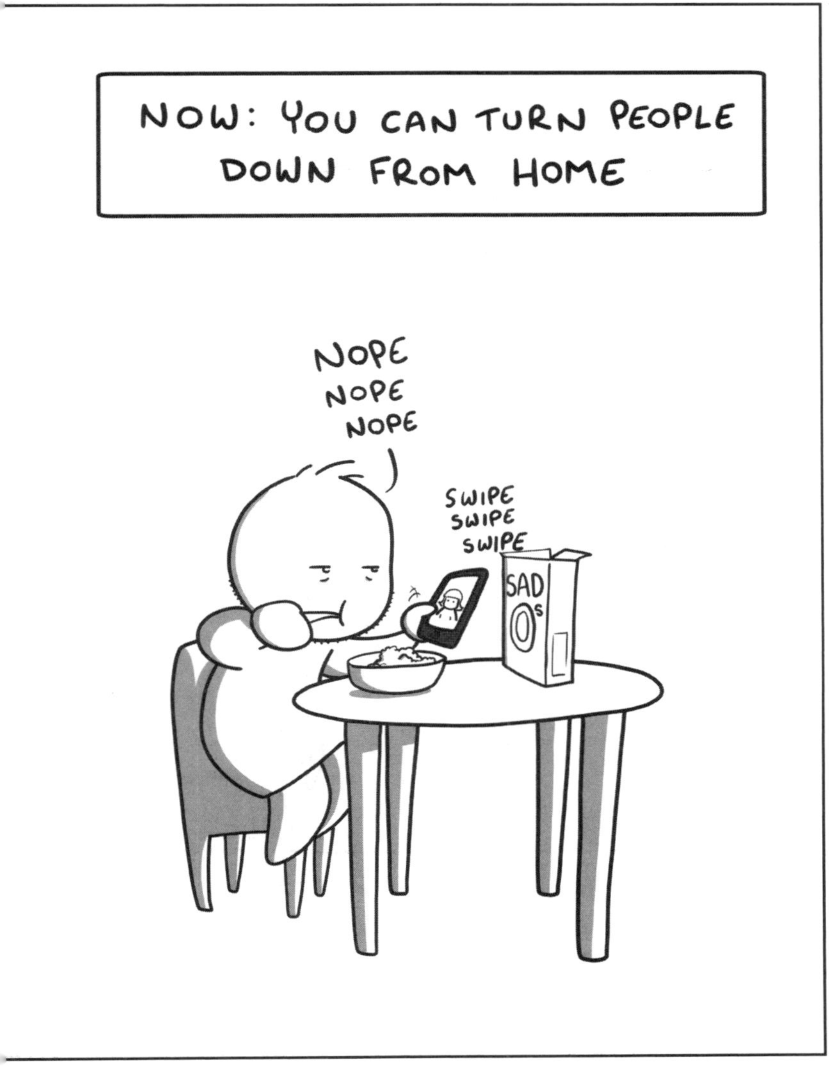
NOW: YOU CAN TURN PEOPLE DOWN FROM HOME
NOPE NOPE NOPE
SWIPE SWIPE SWIPE
SAD Os

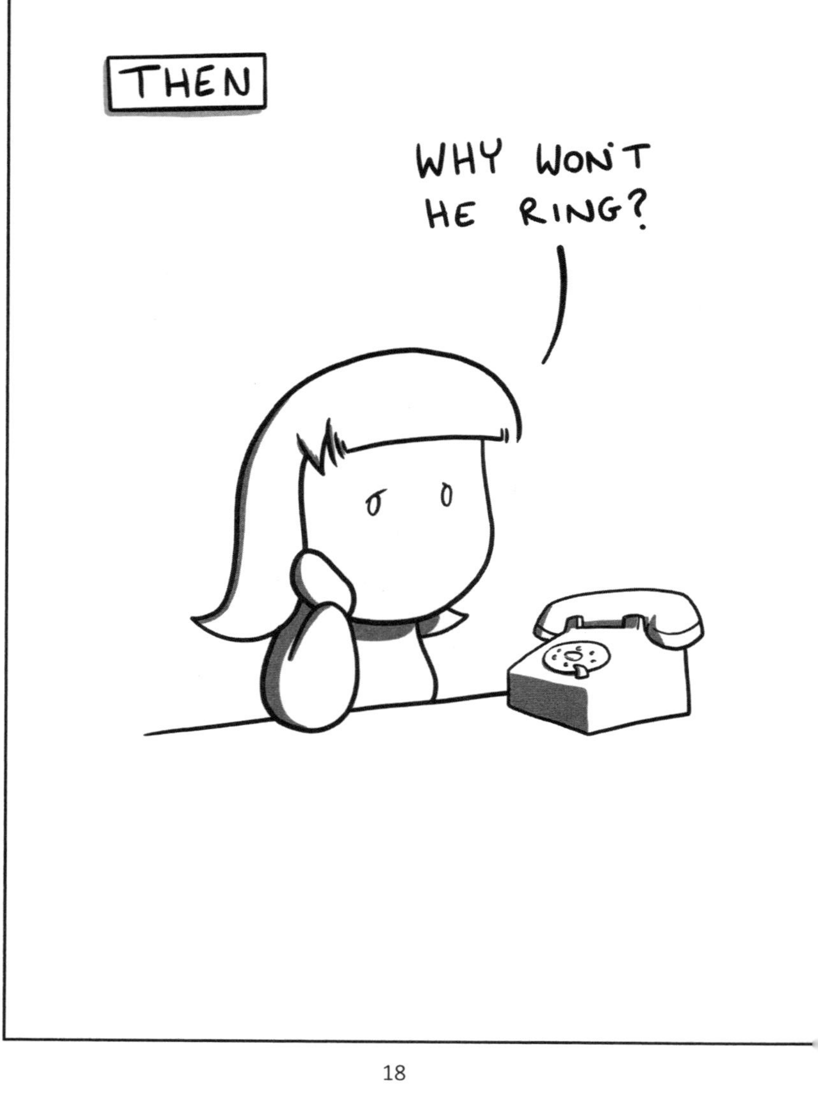
THEN
WHY WON'T HE RING?

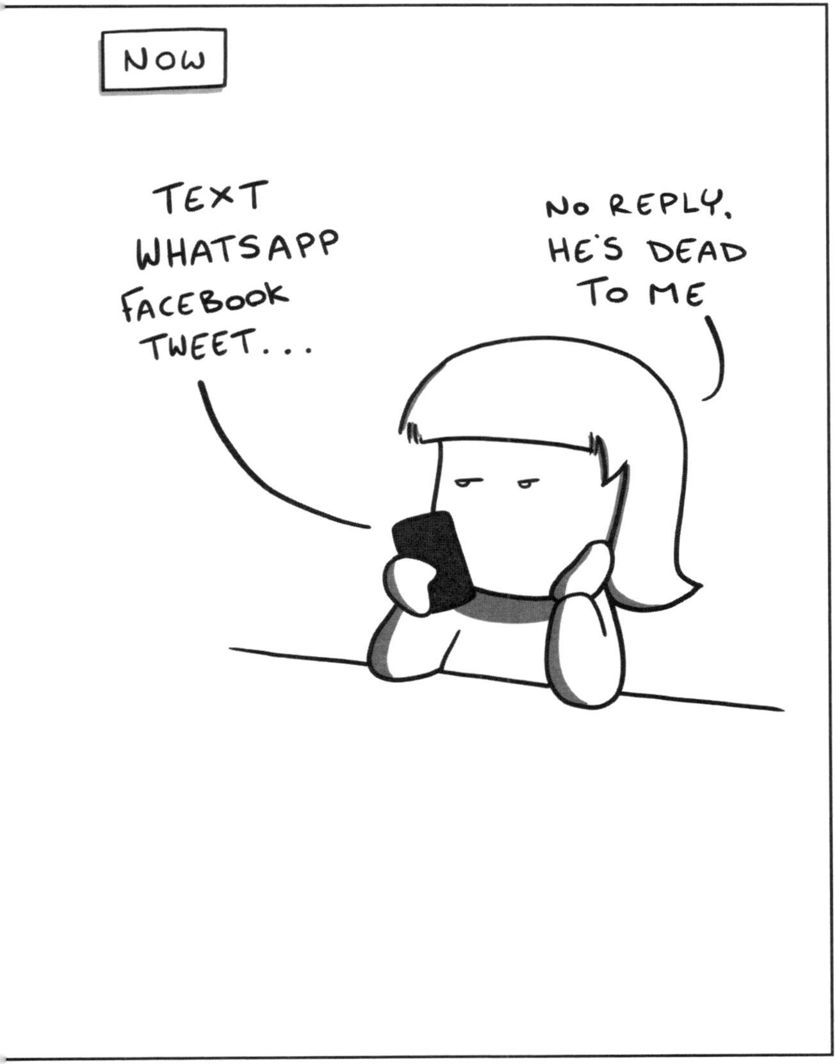
NOW
TEXT
WHATSAPP
FACEBOOK
TWEET...
NO REPLY.
HE'S DEAD
TO ME

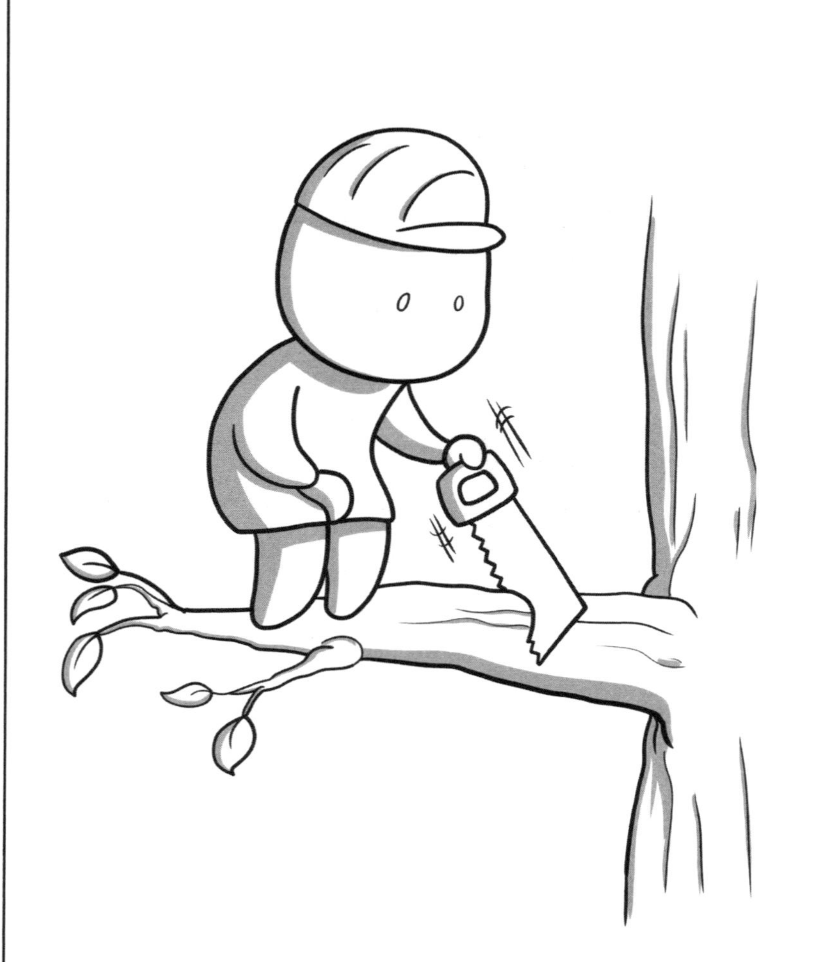

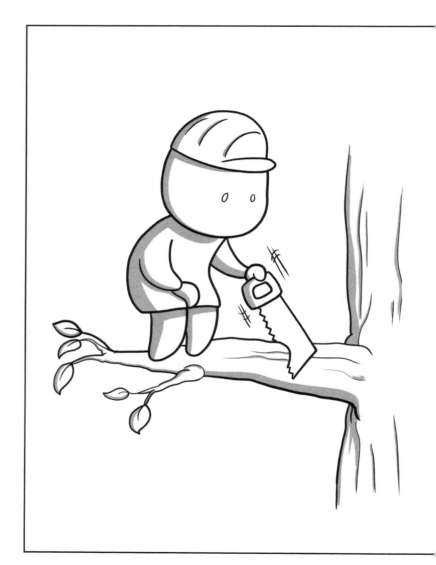

HEALTH AND SAFETY

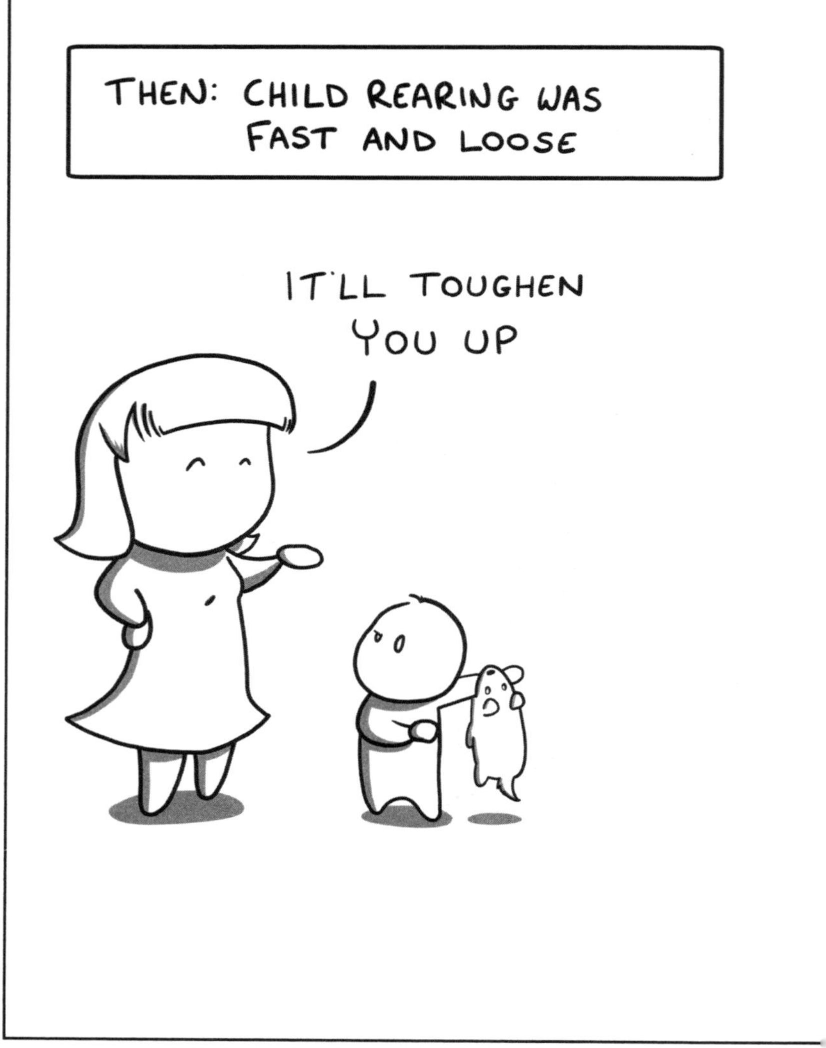
THEN: CHILD REARING WAS FAST AND LOOSE
IT'LL TOUGHEN YOU UP

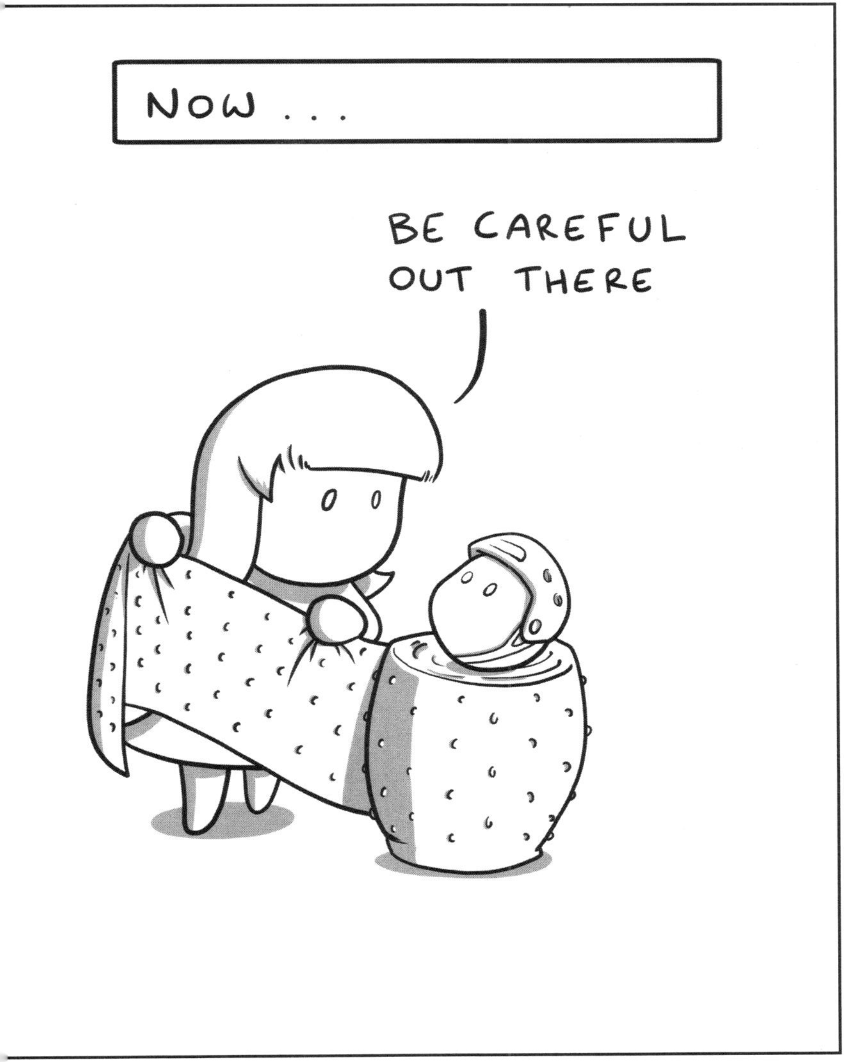
NOW . . .
BE CAREFUL OUT THERE

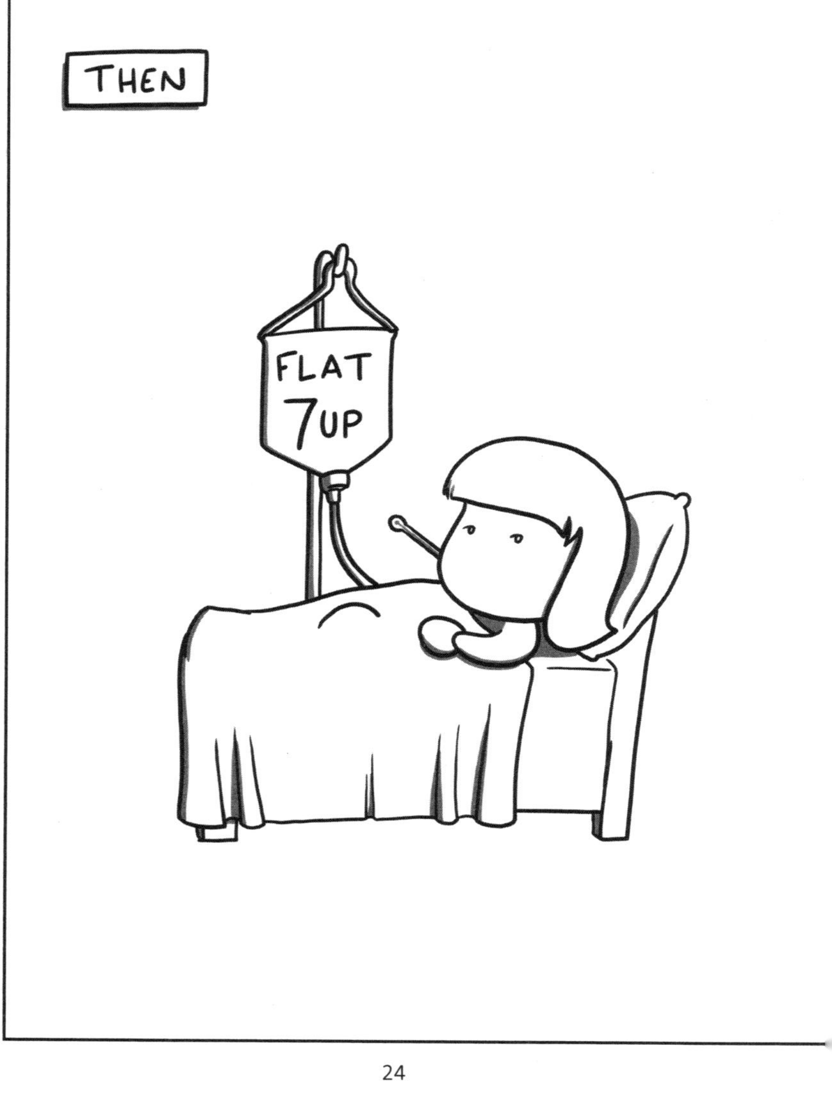
THEN
FLAT
7UP

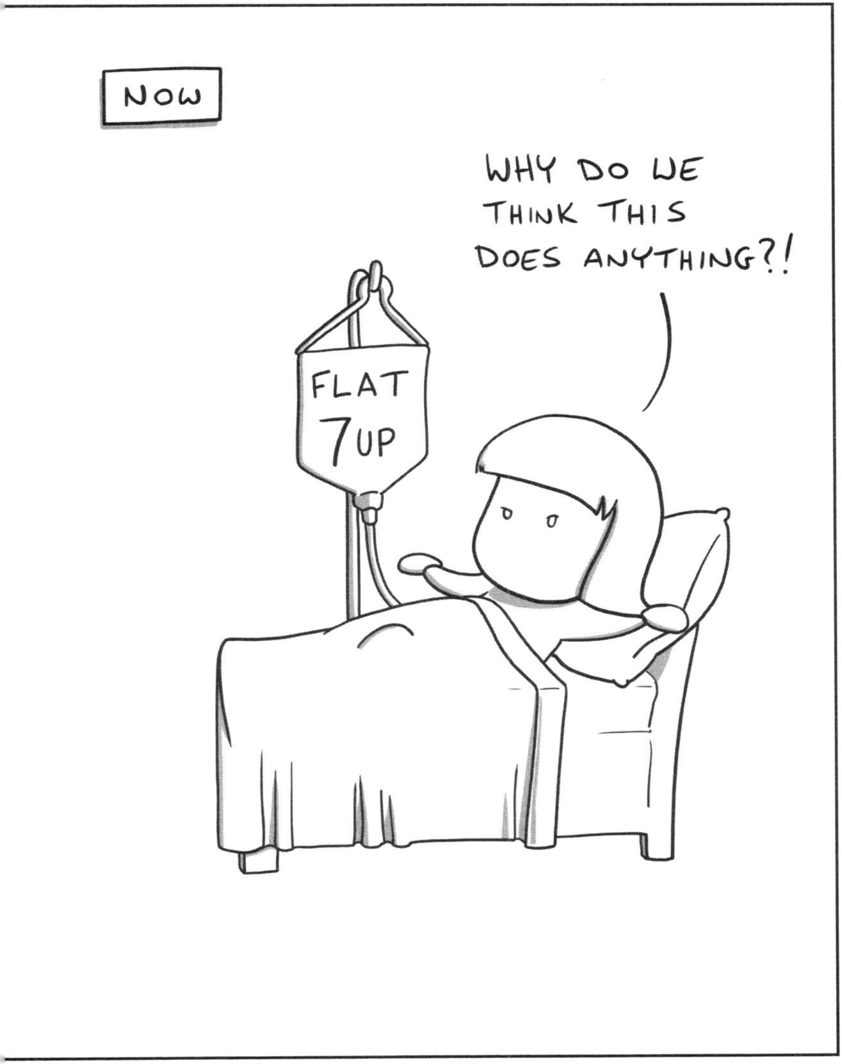
NOW
WHY DO WE THINK THIS DOES ANYTHING?!
FLAT 7UP

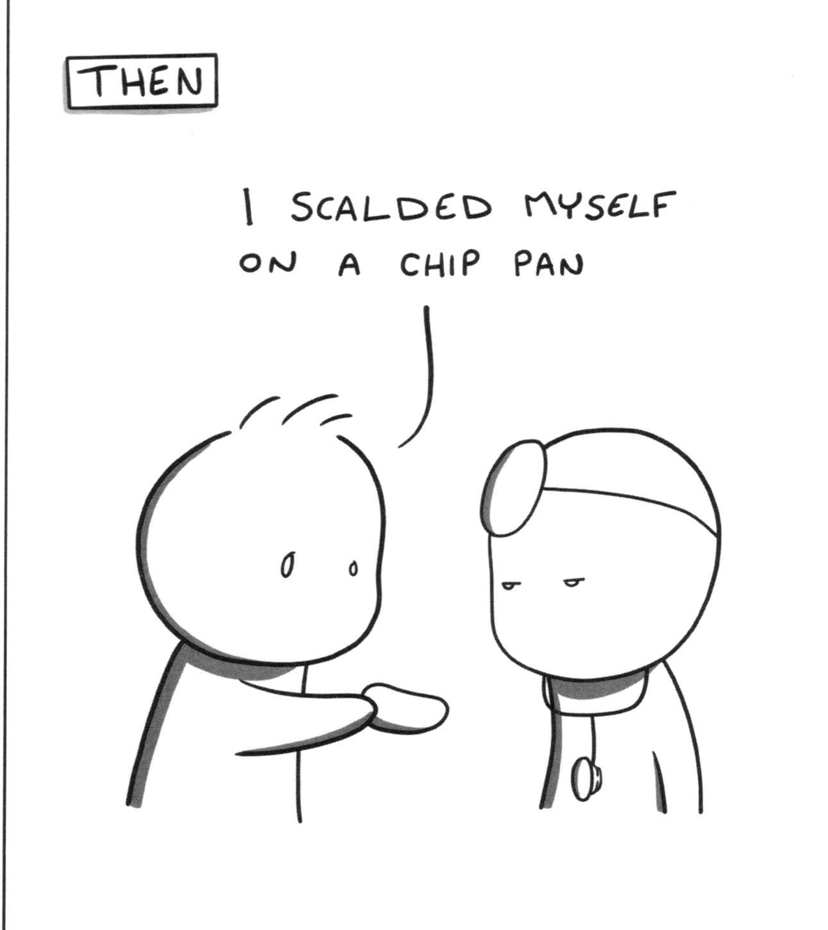
THEN
I SCALDED MYSELF ON A CHIP PAN

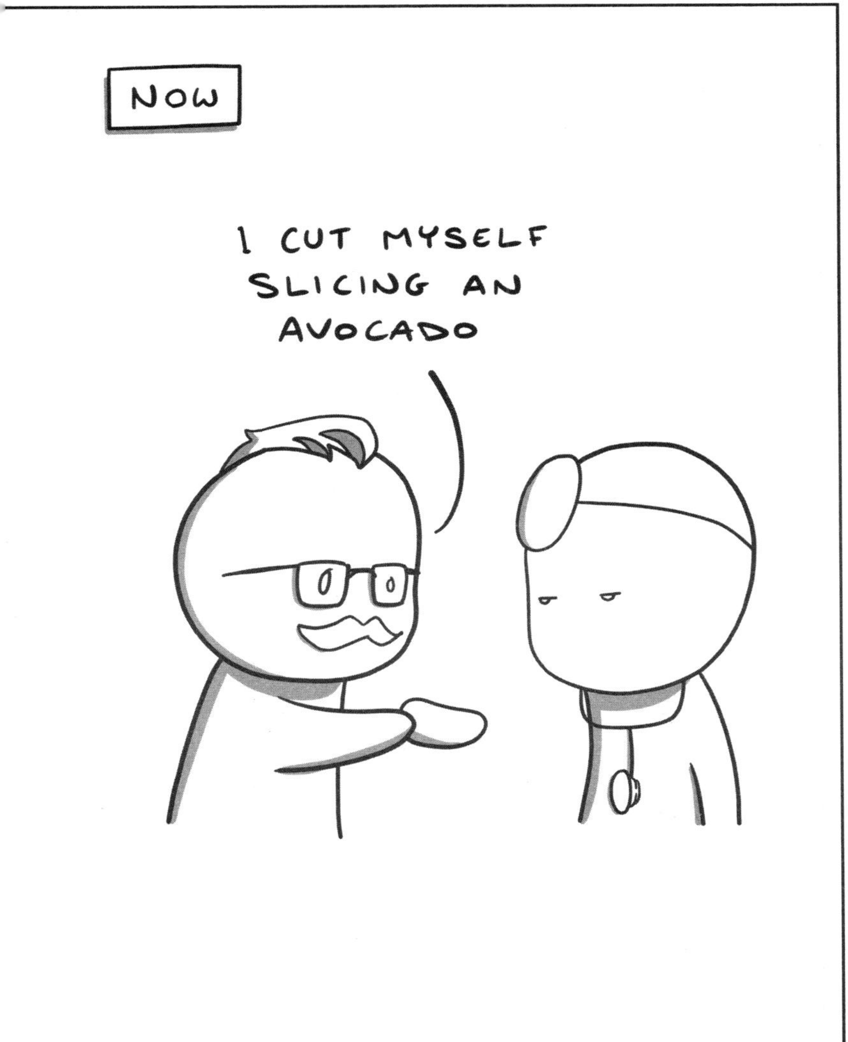
NOW
I CUT MYSELF SLICING AN AVOCADO

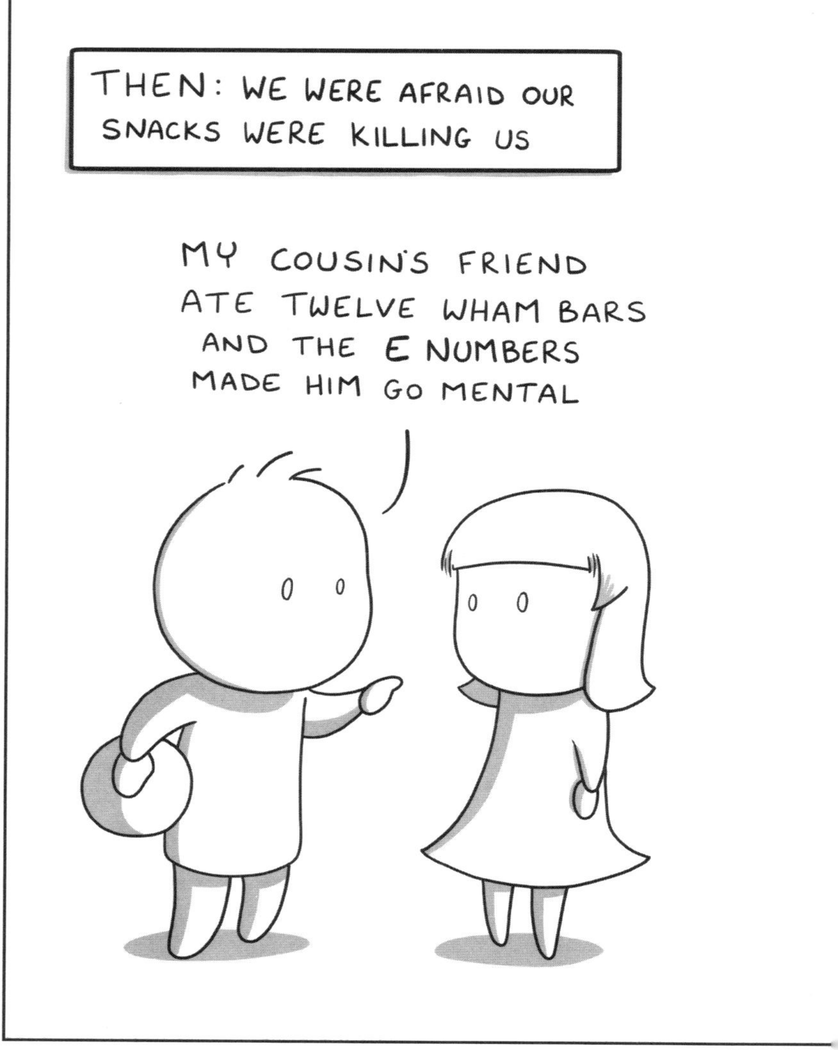
THEN: WE WERE AFRAID OUR SNACKS WERE KILLING US
MY COUSIN'S FRIEND ATE TWELVE WHAM BARS AND THE E NUMBERS MADE HIM GO MENTAL

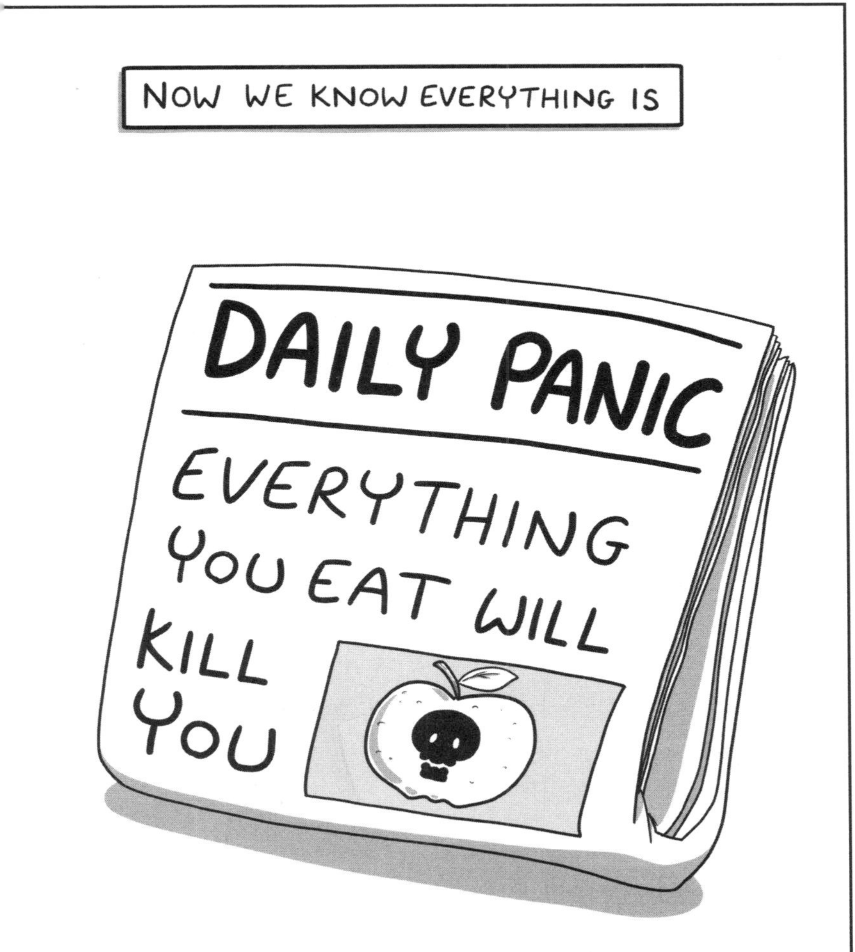
NOW WE KNOW EVERYTHING IS
DAILY PANIC
EVERYTHING YOU EAT WILL KILL YOU

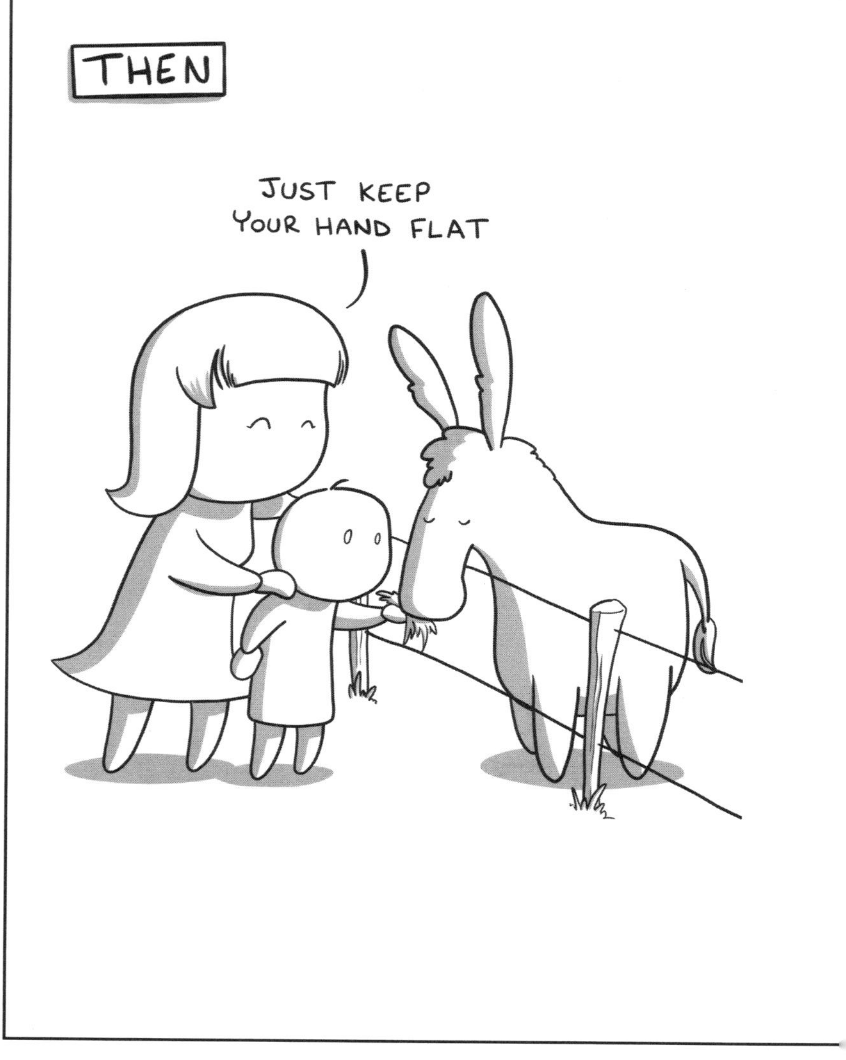
THEN
JUST KEEP YOUR HAND FLAT

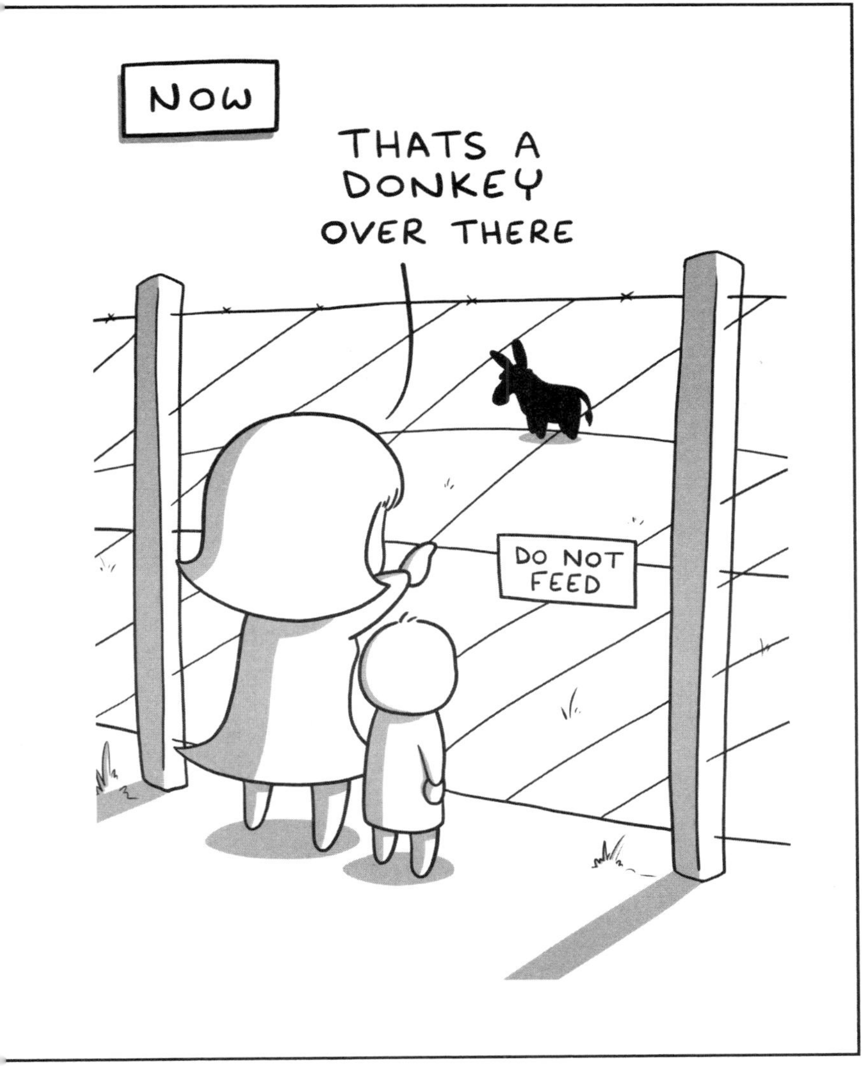
NOW
THATS A DONKEY OVER THERE
DO NOT FEED

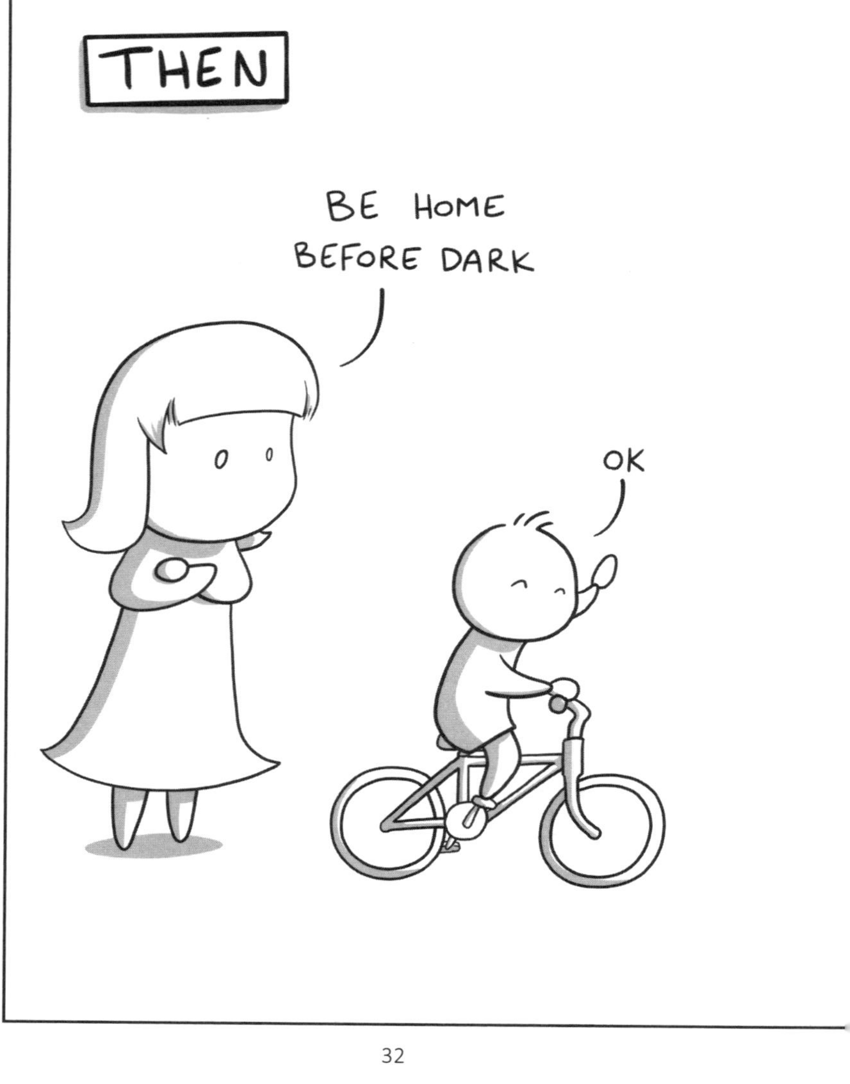
THEN
BE HOME BEFORE DARK
OK

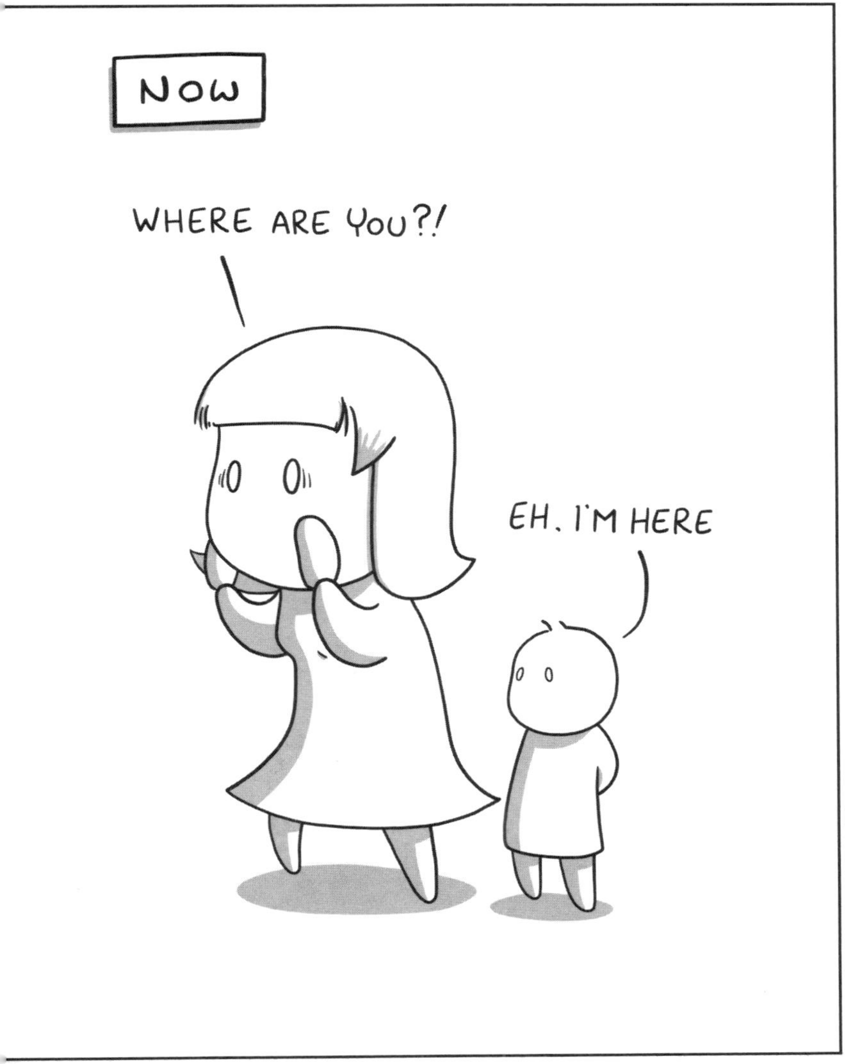
NOW
WHERE ARE YOU?!
EH. I'M HERE

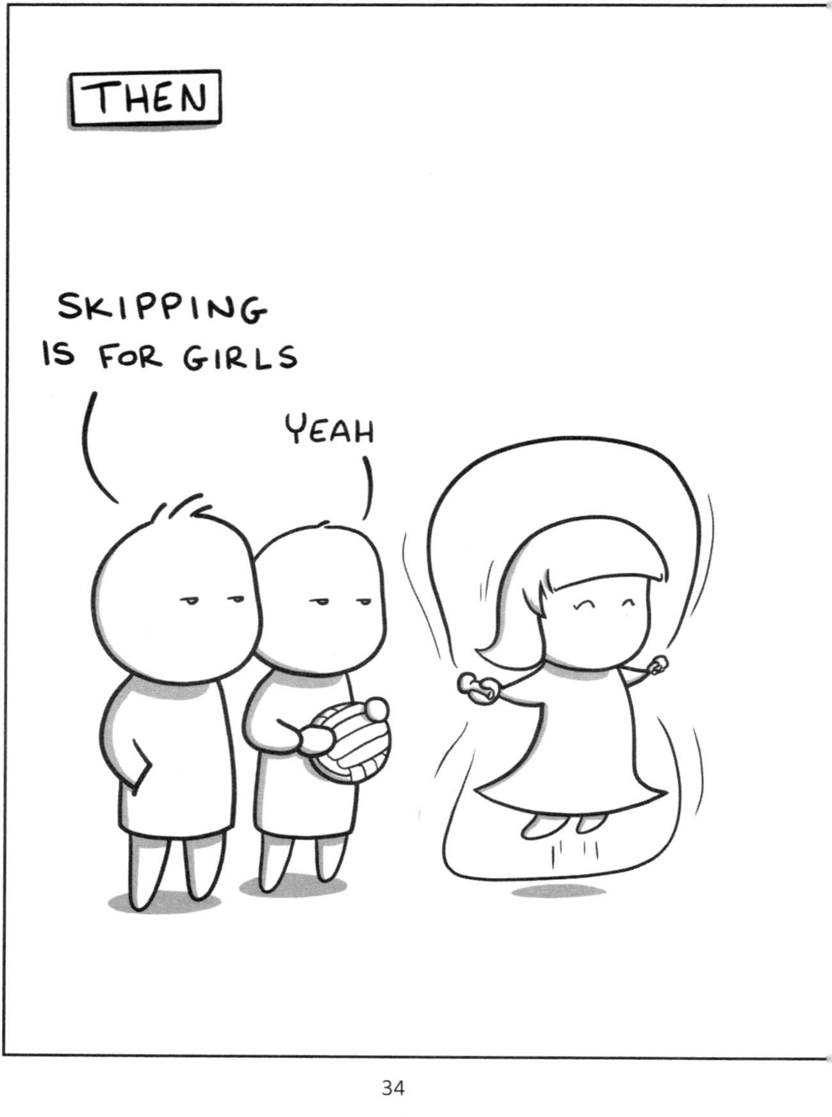
THEN
SKIPPING IS FOR GIRLS
YEAH

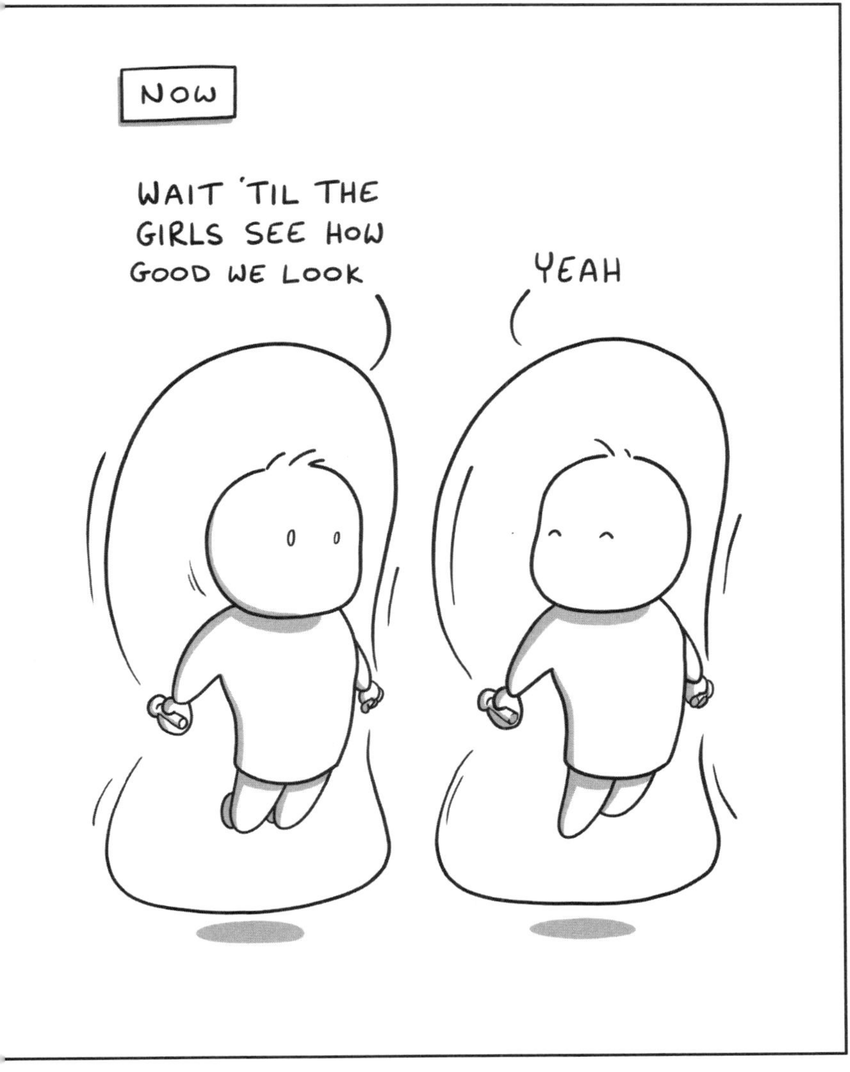
NOW
WAIT 'TIL THE GIRLS SEE HOW GOOD WE LOOK
YEAH

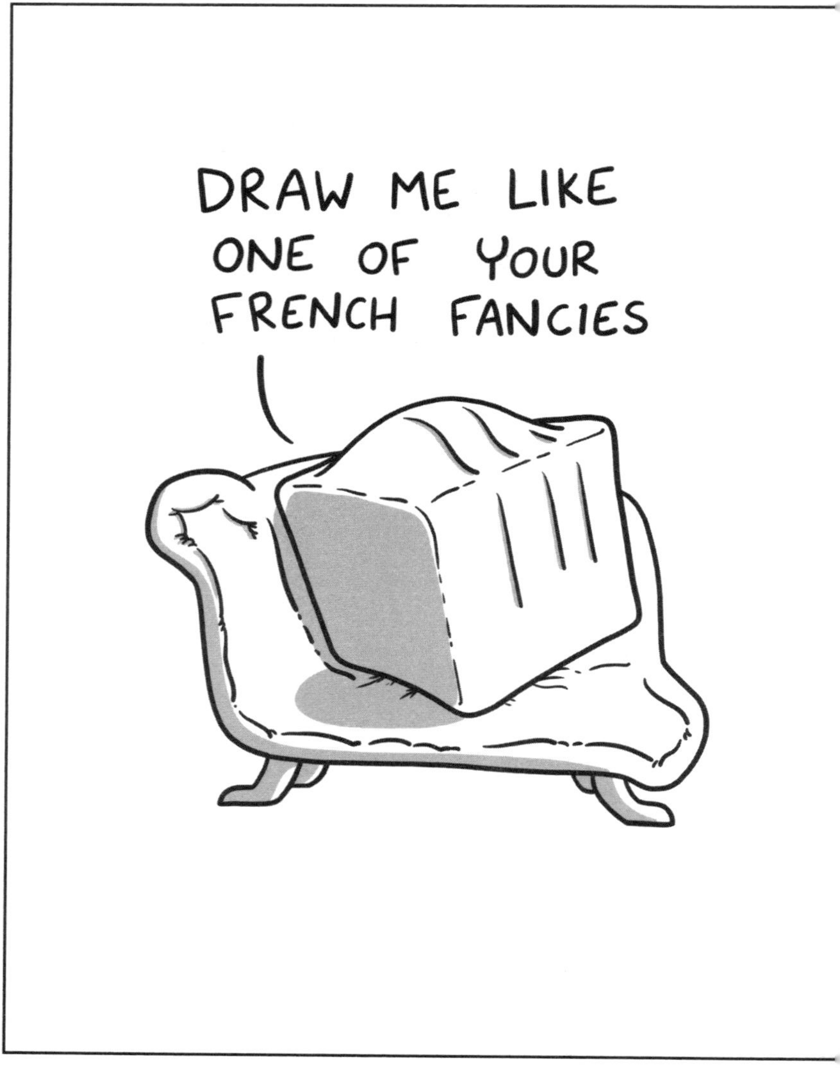
DRAW ME LIKE ONE OF YOUR FRENCH FANCIES

FOOD

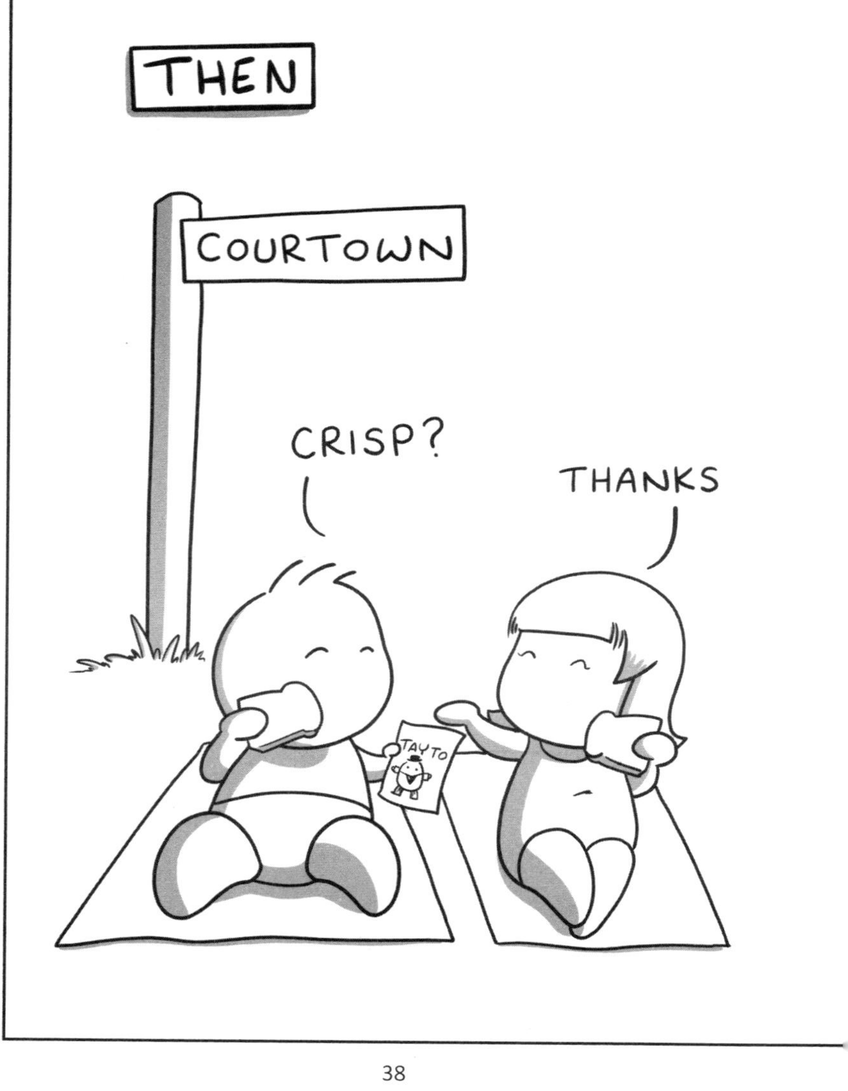
THEN
COURTOWN
CRISP?
THANKS
TAYTO

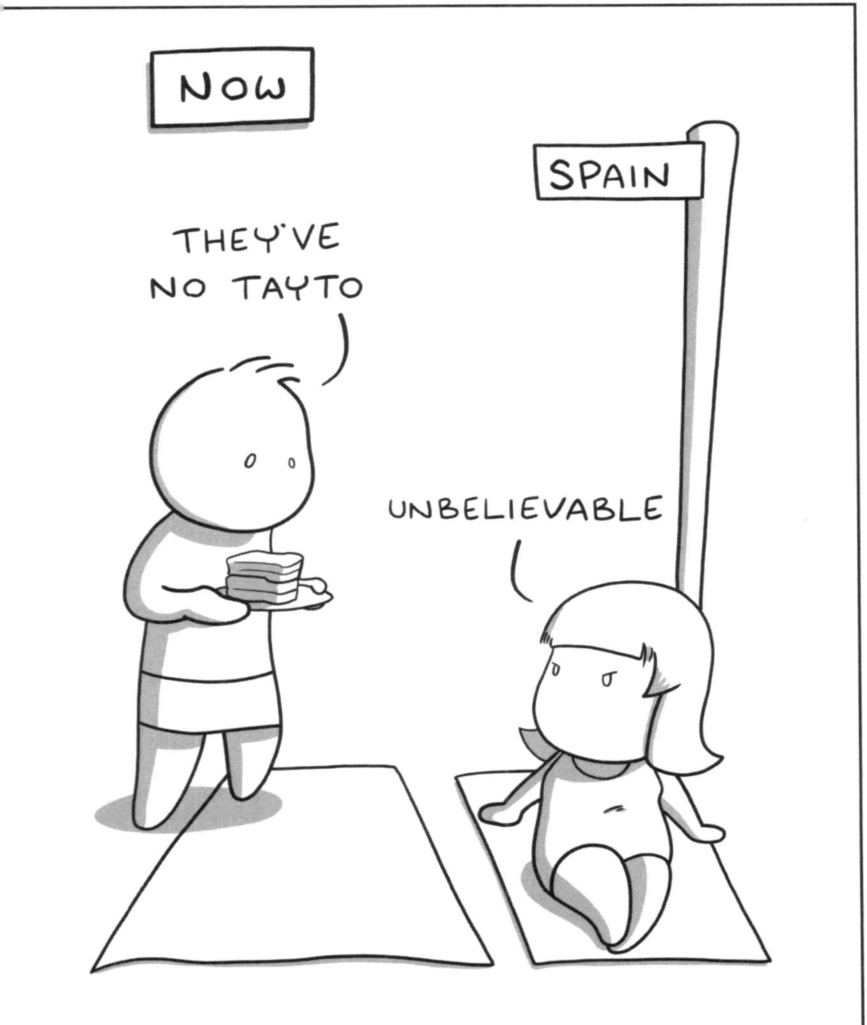
NOW
SPAIN
THEY'VE NO TAYTO
UNBELIEVABLE

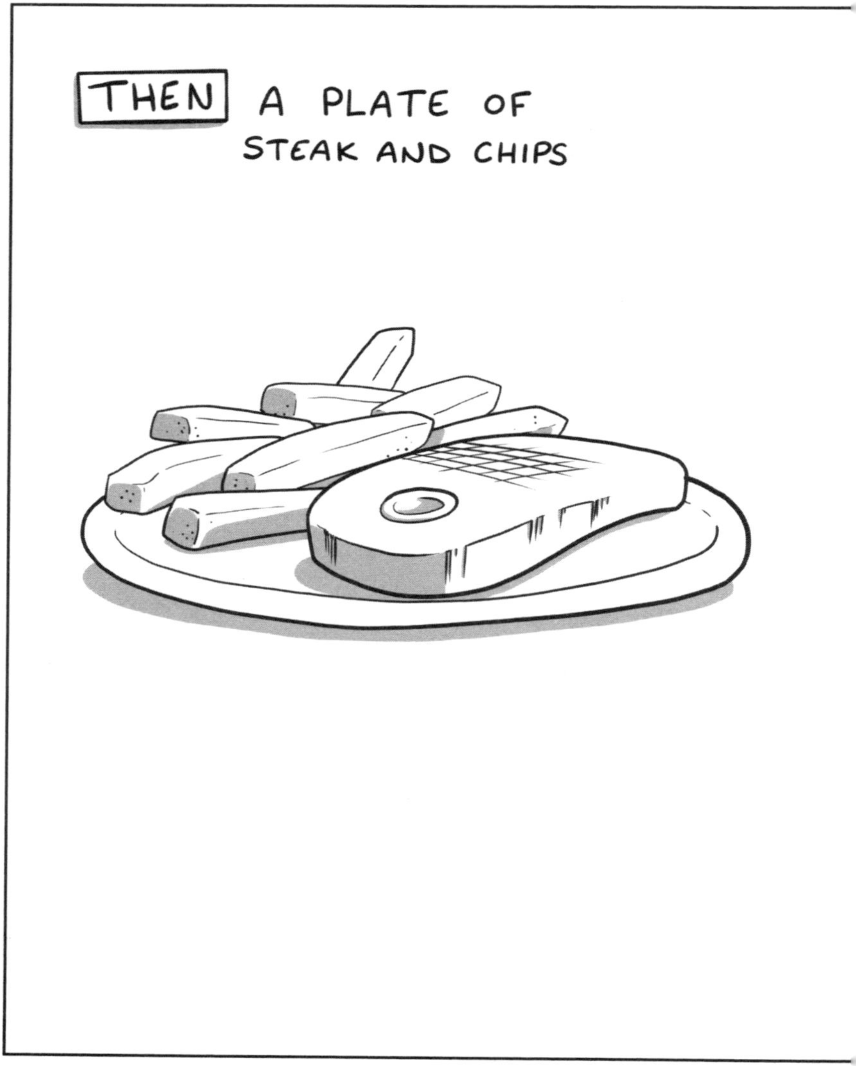
THEN A PLATE OF
STEAK AND CHIPS

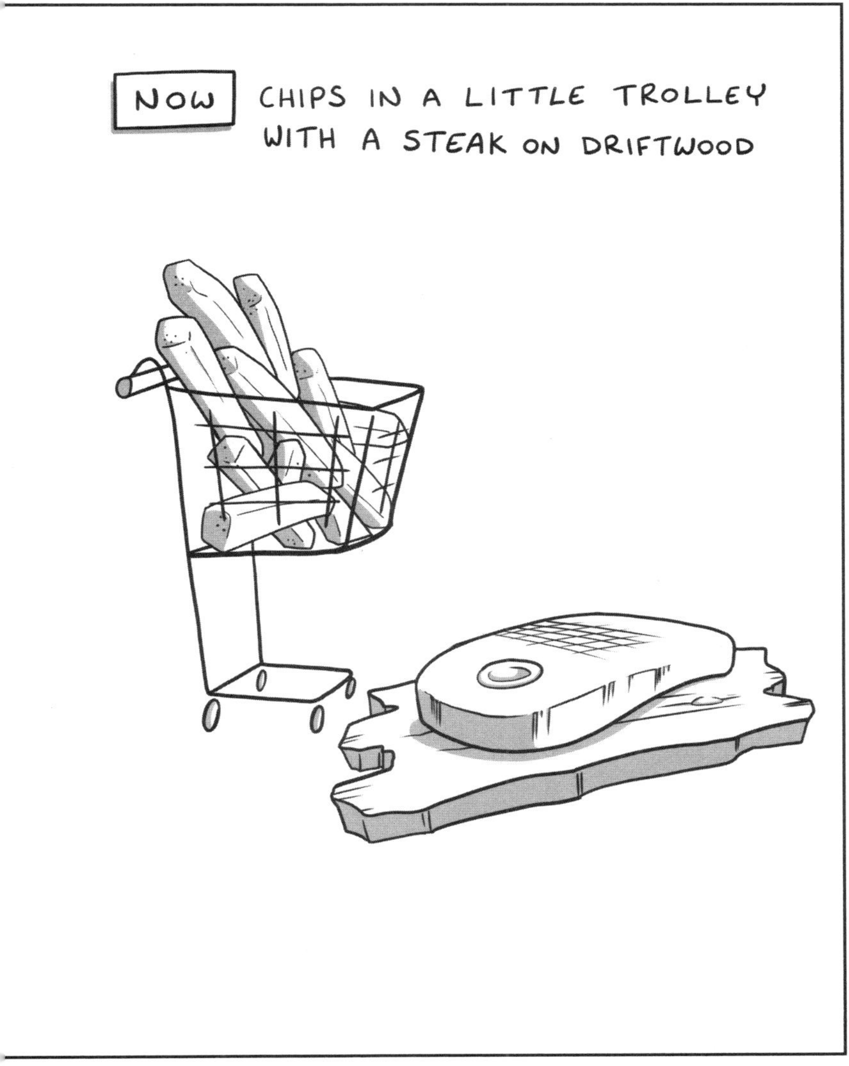
NOW
CHIPS IN A LITTLE TROLLEY
WITH A STEAK ON DRIFTWOOD

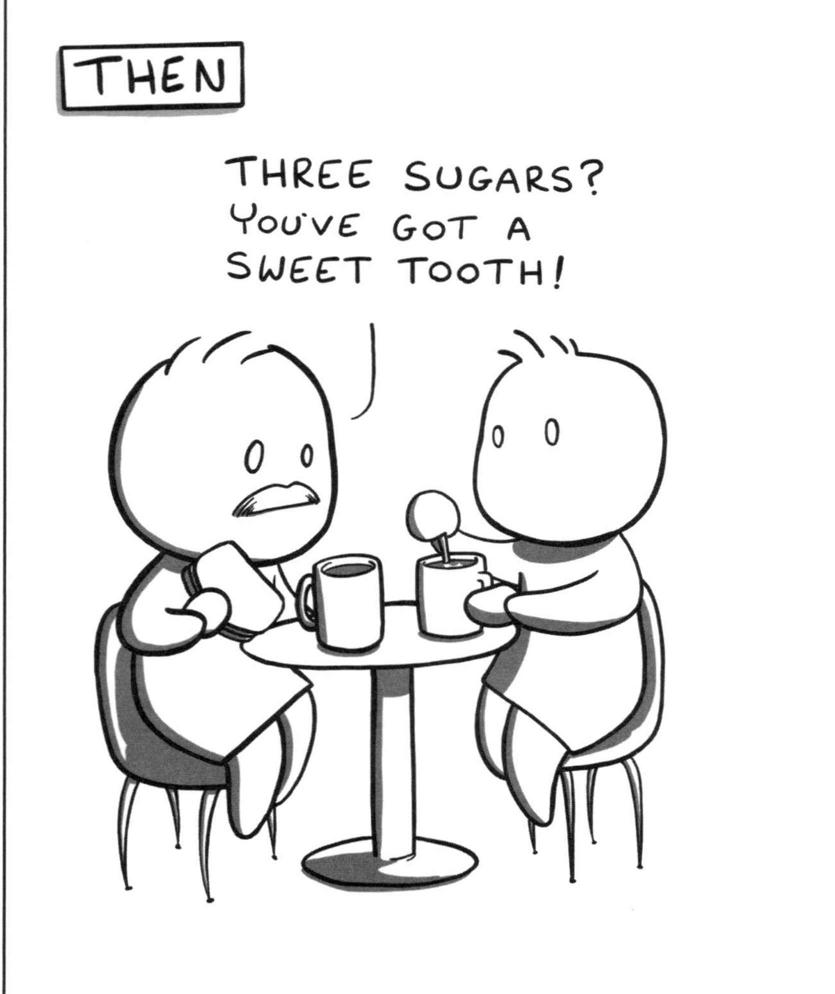
THEN
THREE SUGARS? YOU'VE GOT A SWEET TOOTH!

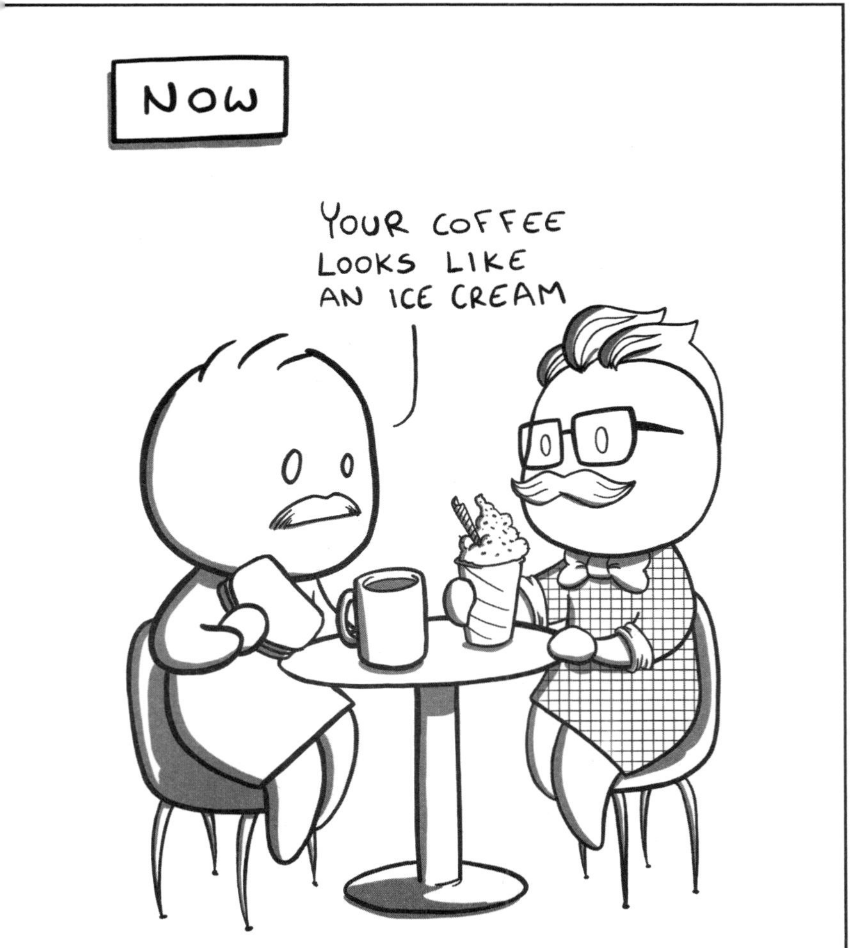
NOW
YOUR COFFEE LOOKS LIKE AN ICE CREAM

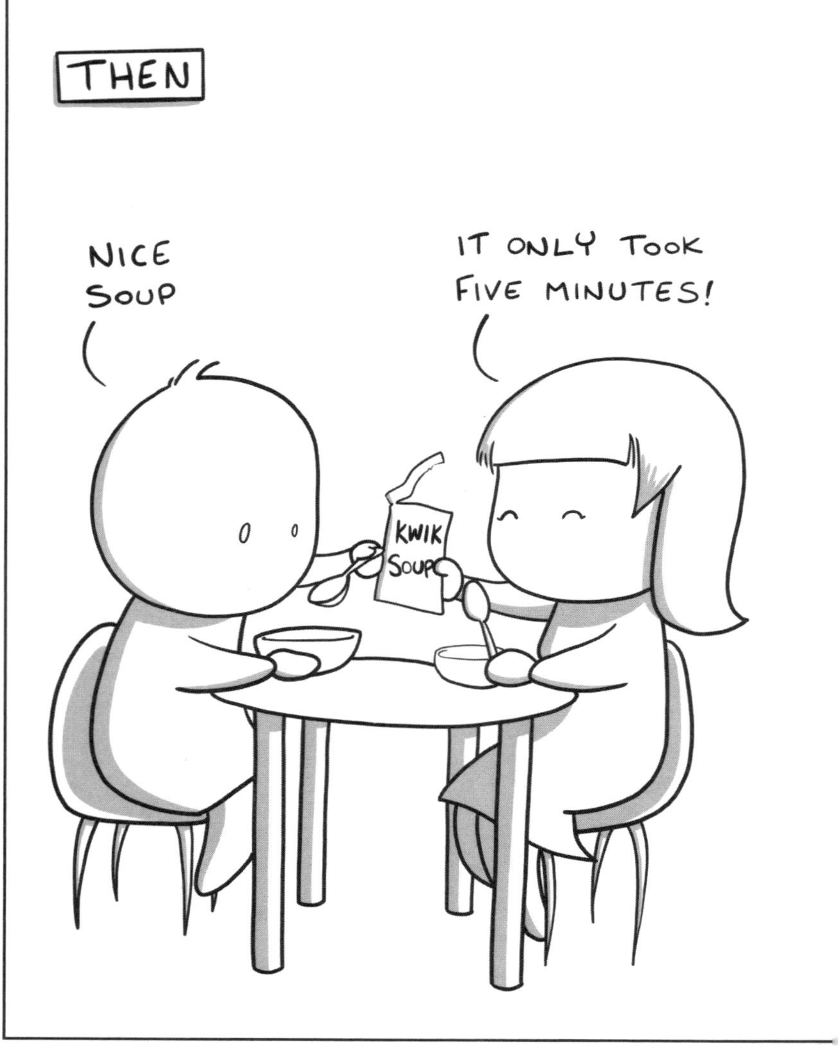
THEN
NICE SOUP
IT ONLY TOOK FIVE MINUTES!
KWIK SOUP

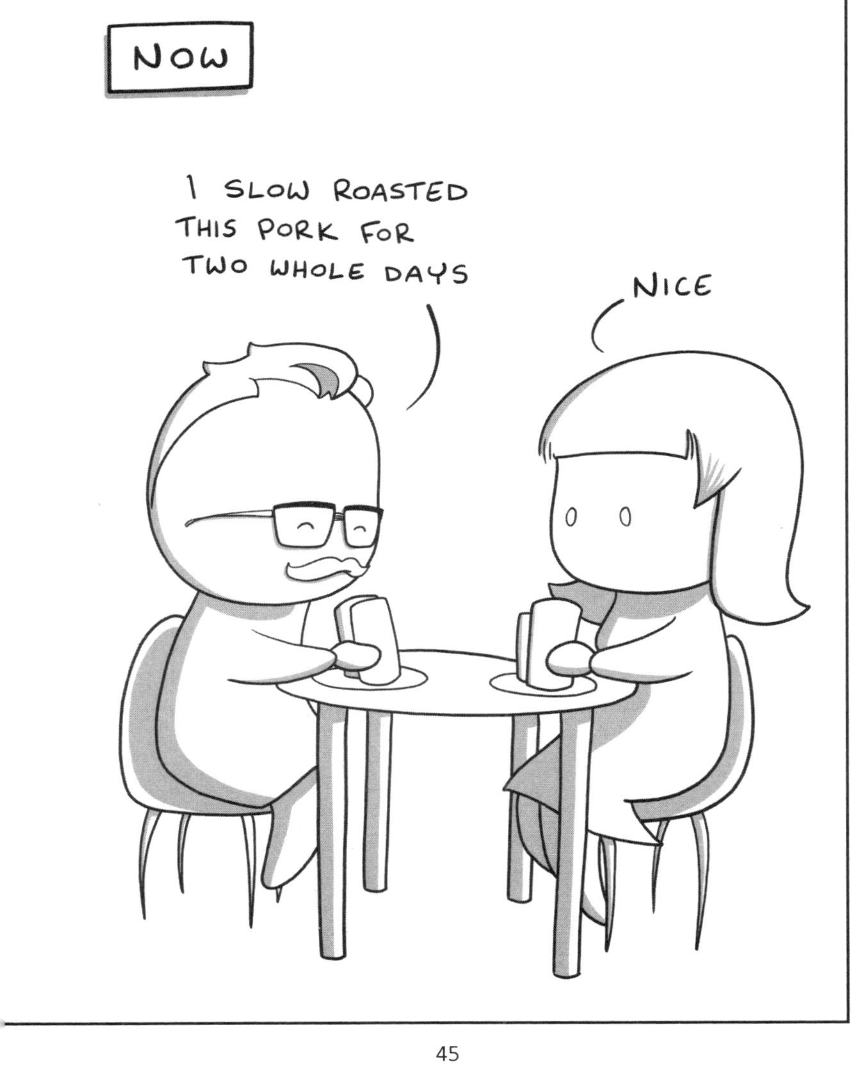
NOW
I SLOW ROASTED THIS PORK FOR TWO WHOLE DAYS
NICE

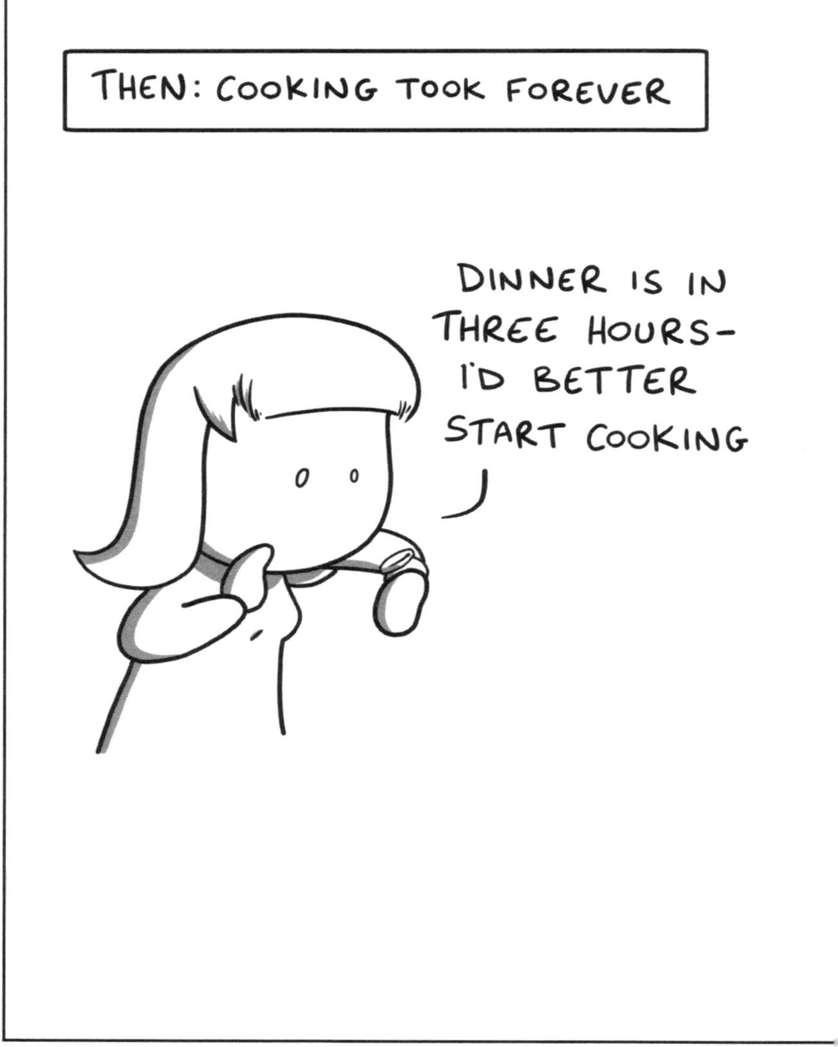
THEN: COOKING TOOK FOREVER
DINNER IS IN THREE HOURS- I'D BETTER START COOKING

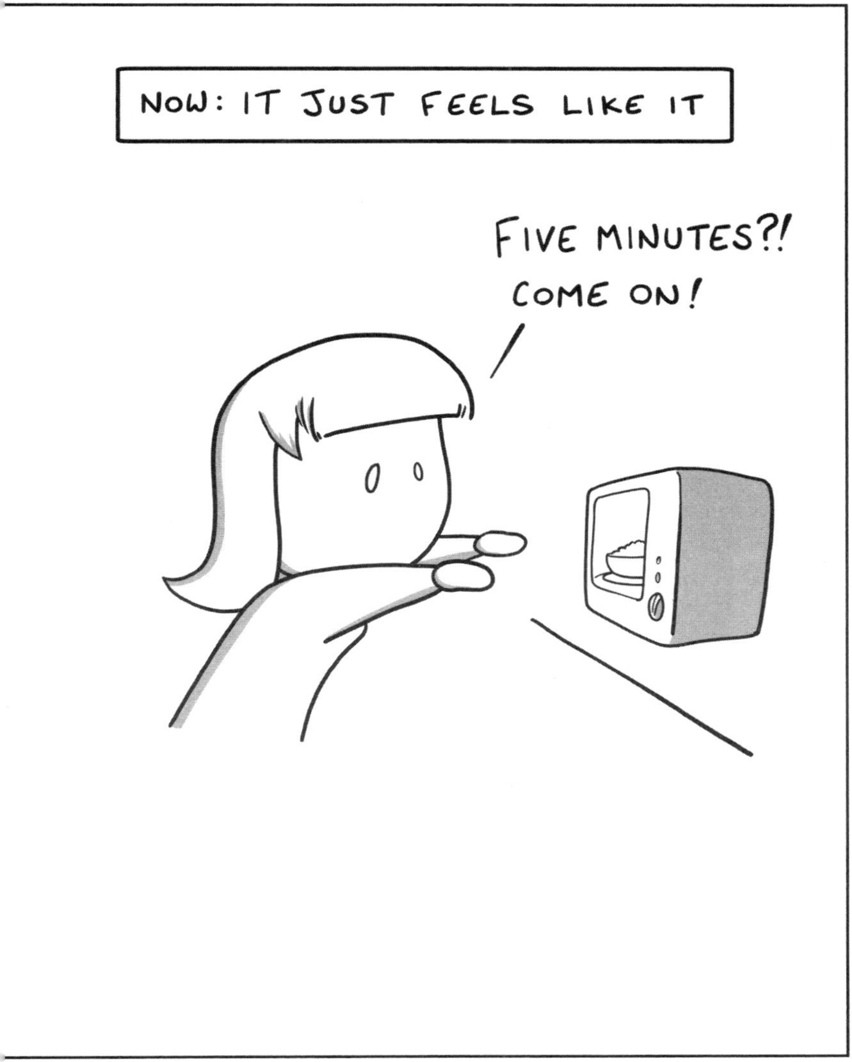
NOW: IT JUST FEELS LIKE IT
FIVE MINUTES?! COME ON!

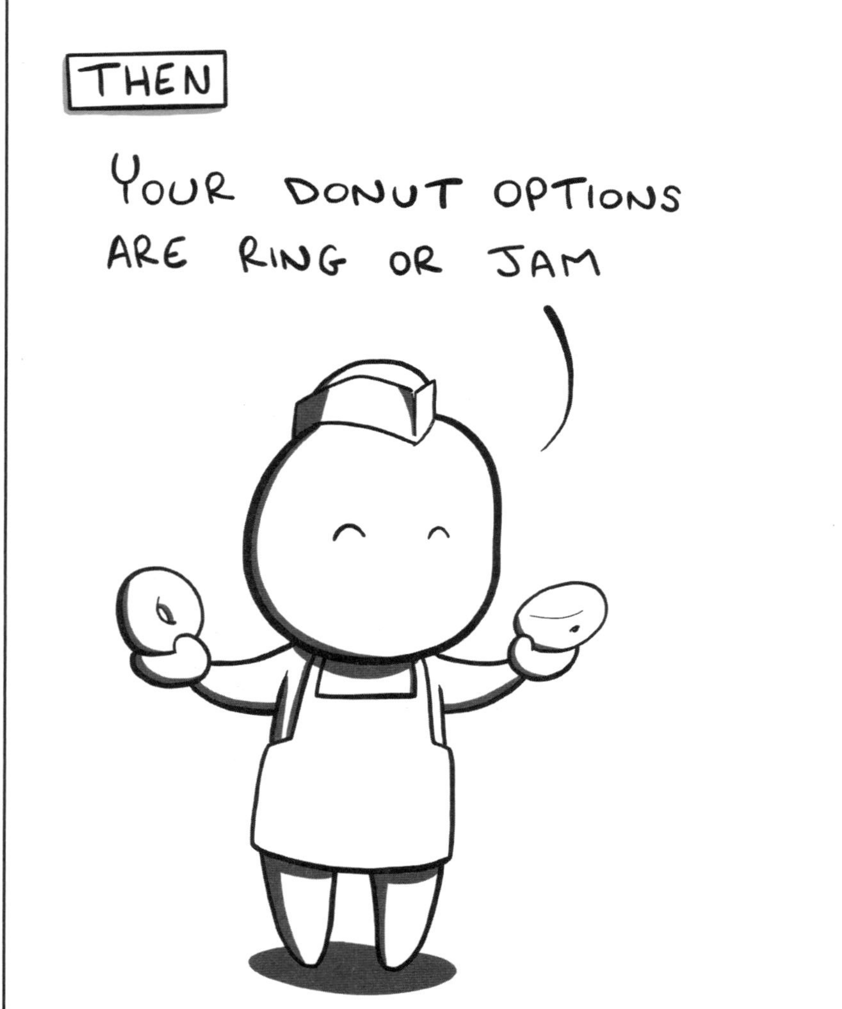
THEN
YOUR DONUT OPTIONS ARE RING OR JAM

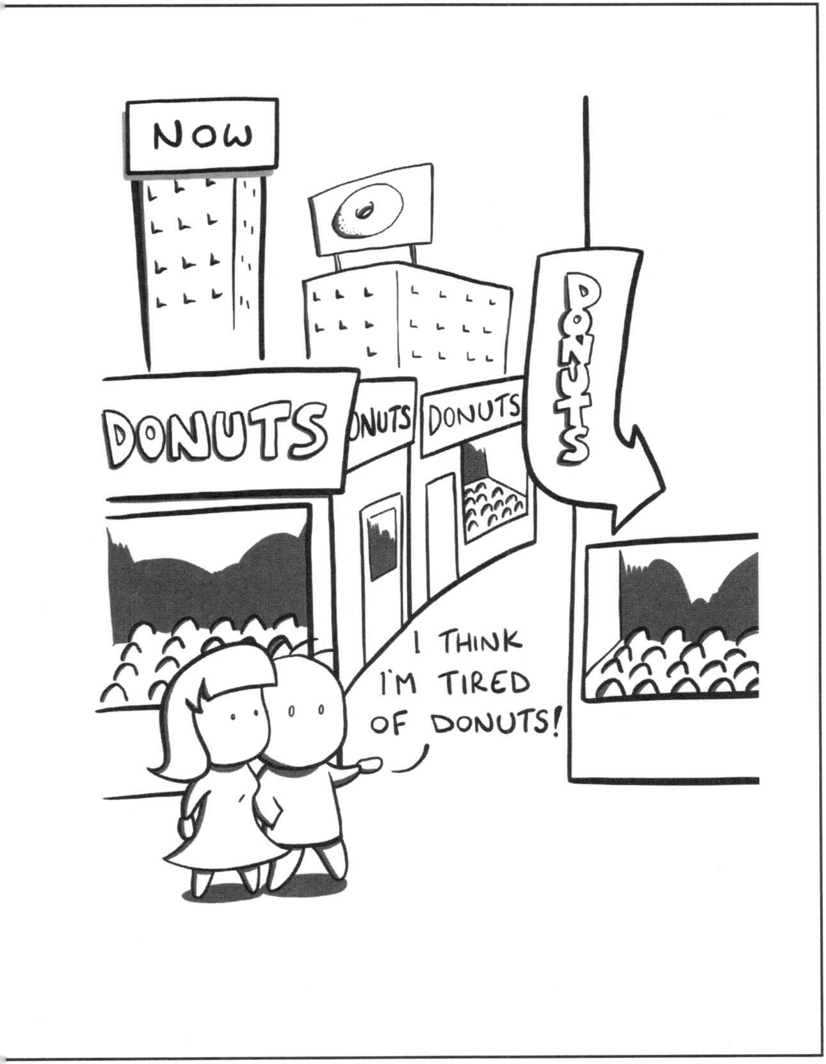
NOW
DONUTS
ONUTS
DONUTS
DONUTS
I THINK I'M TIRED OF DONUTS!

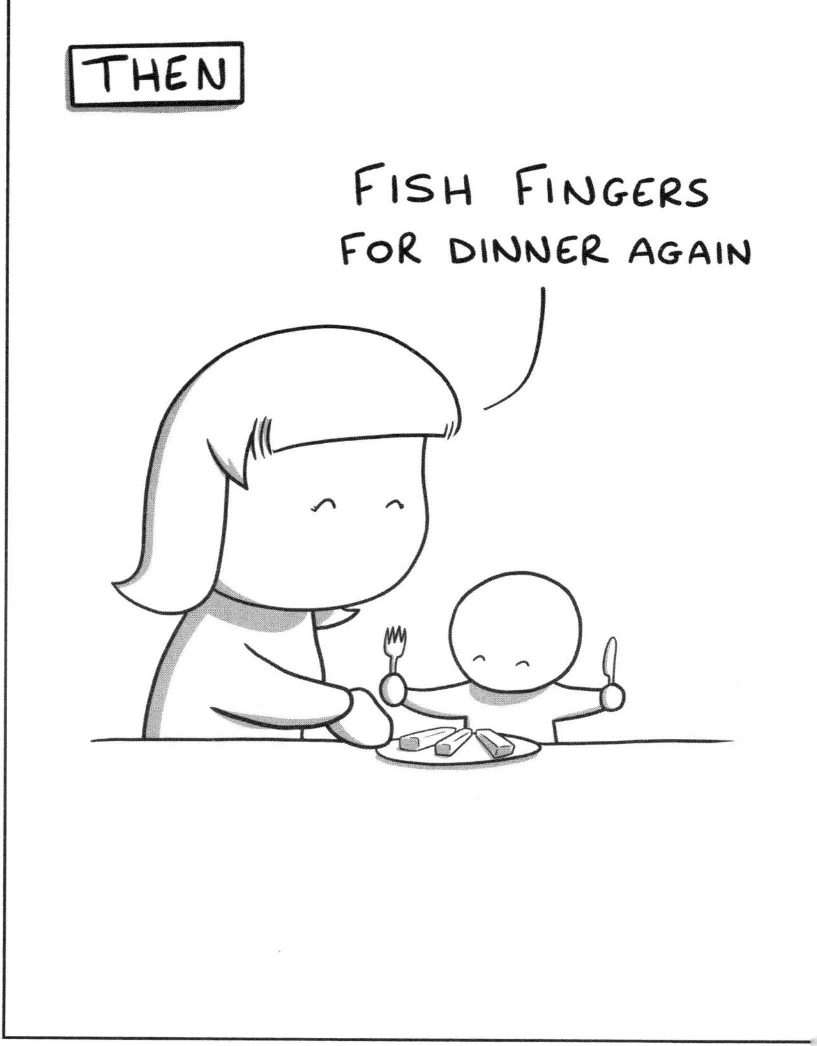
THEN
FISH FINGERS FOR DINNER AGAIN

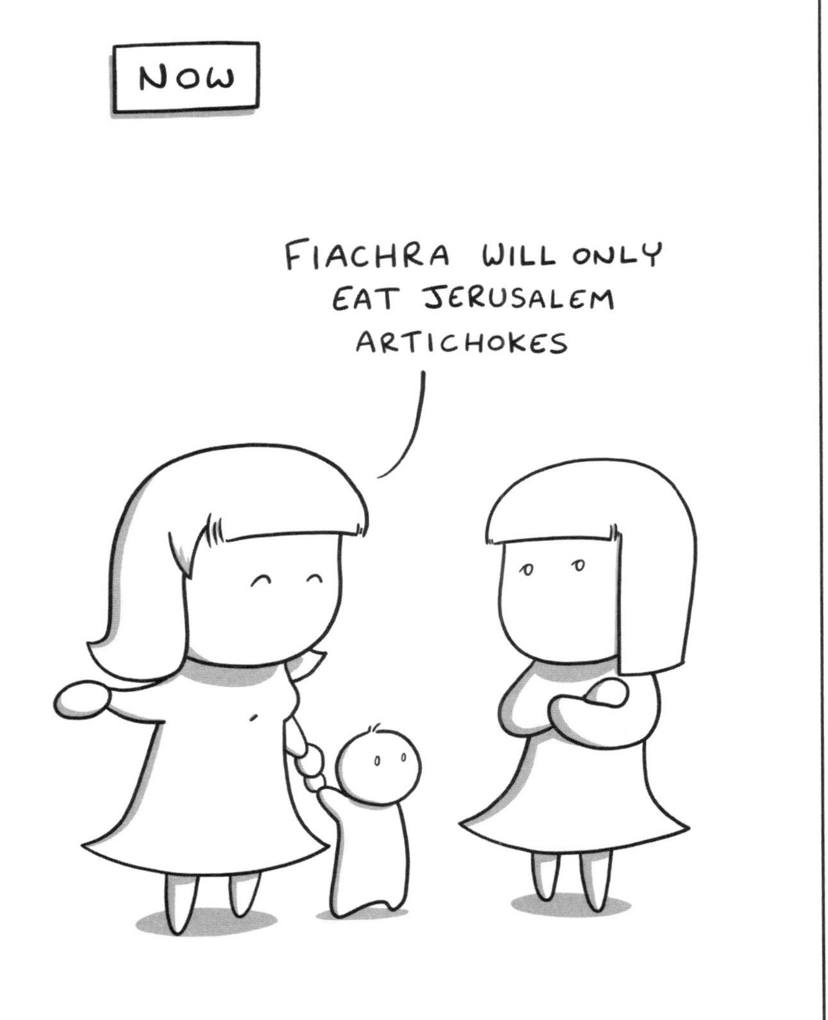
NOW
FIACHRA WILL ONLY EAT JERUSALEM ARTICHOKES

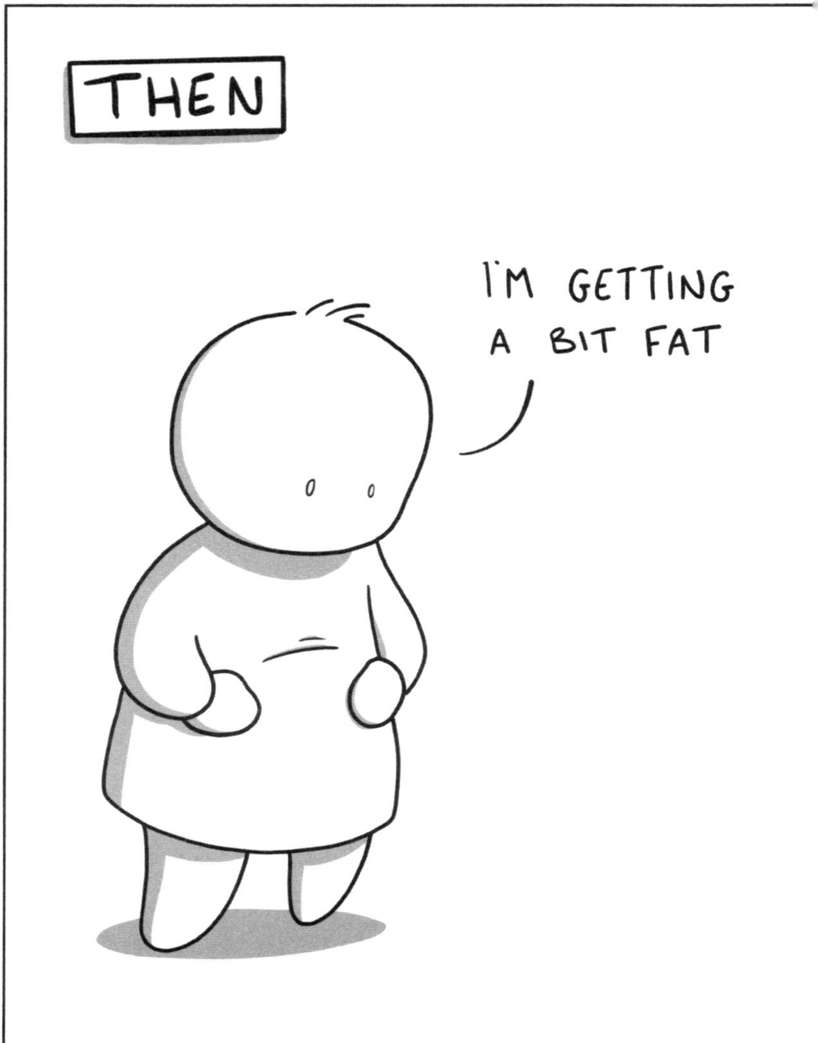
THEN
I'M GETTING A BIT FAT

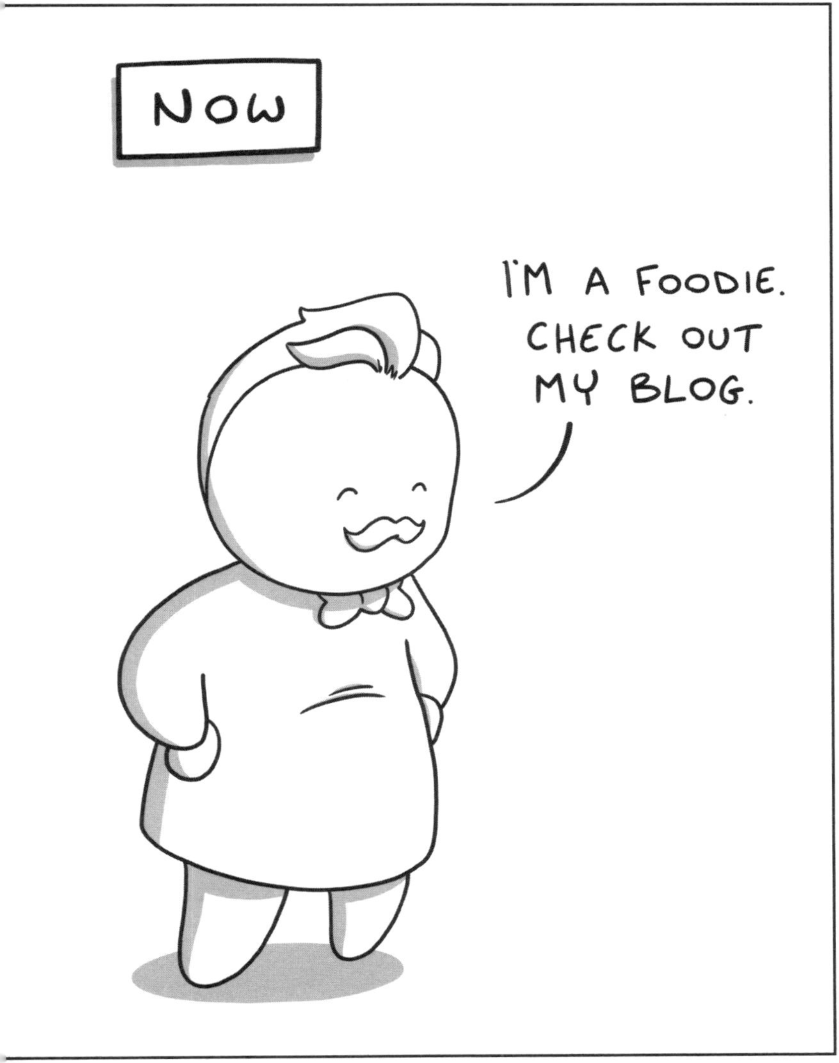
NOW
I'M A FOODIE. CHECK OUT MY BLOG.

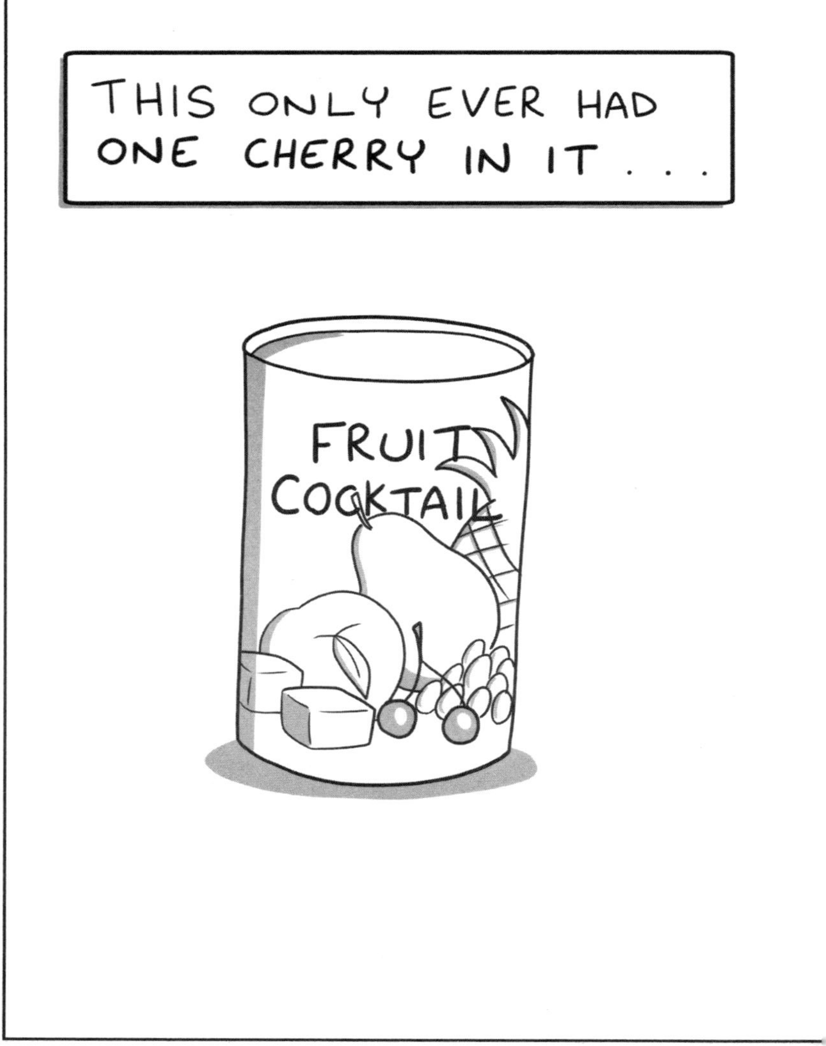
THIS ONLY EVER HAD ONE CHERRY IN IT . . .
FRUIT COCKTAIL

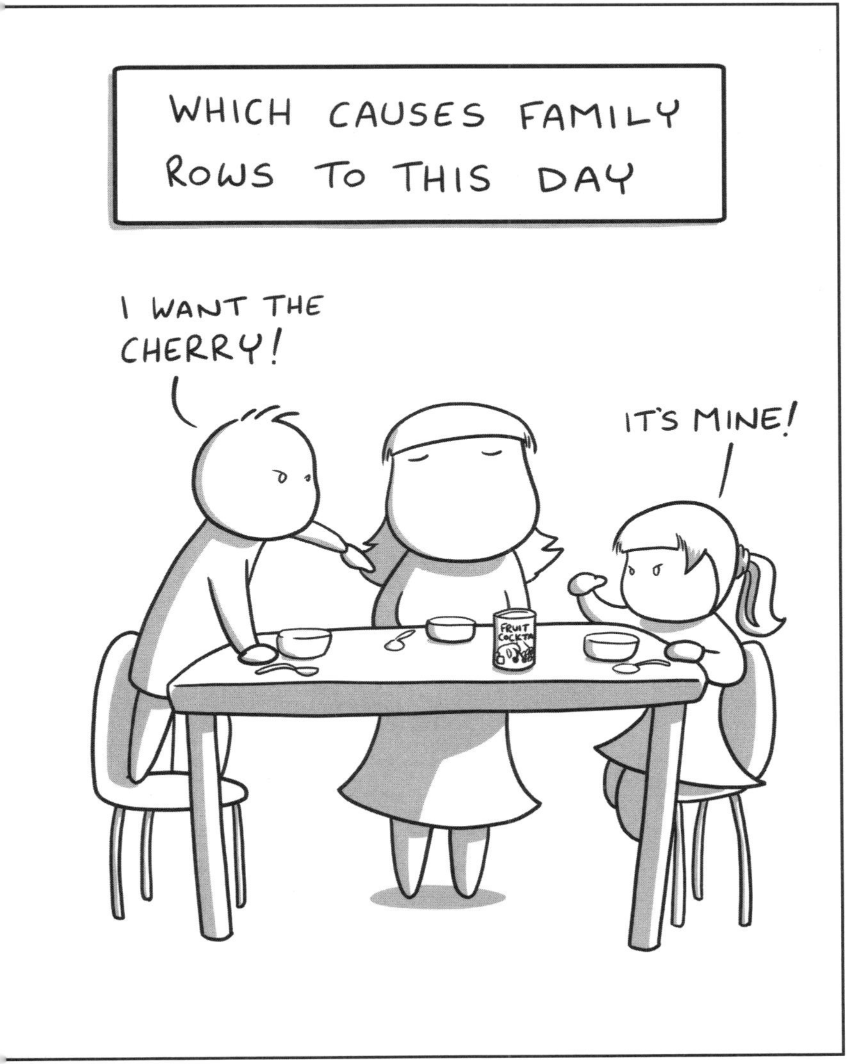
WHICH CAUSES FAMILY ROWS TO THIS DAY
I WANT THE CHERRY!
IT'S MINE!

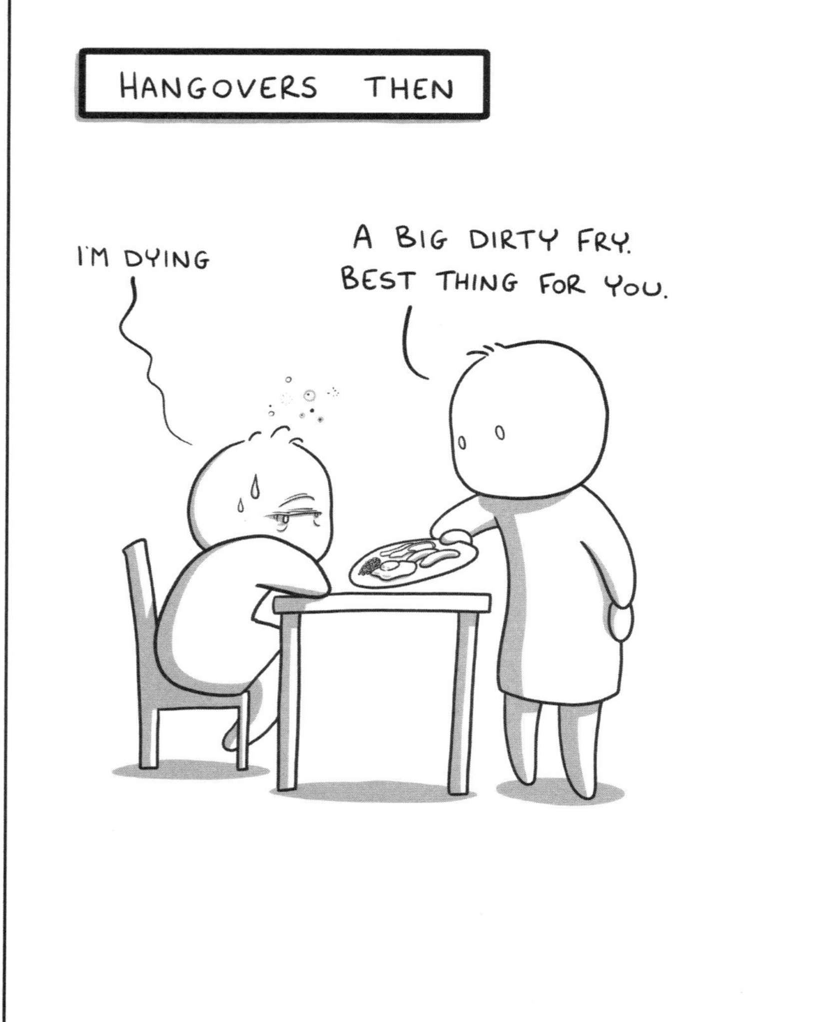
HANGOVERS THEN
I'M DYING
A BIG DIRTY FRY.
BEST THING FOR YOU.

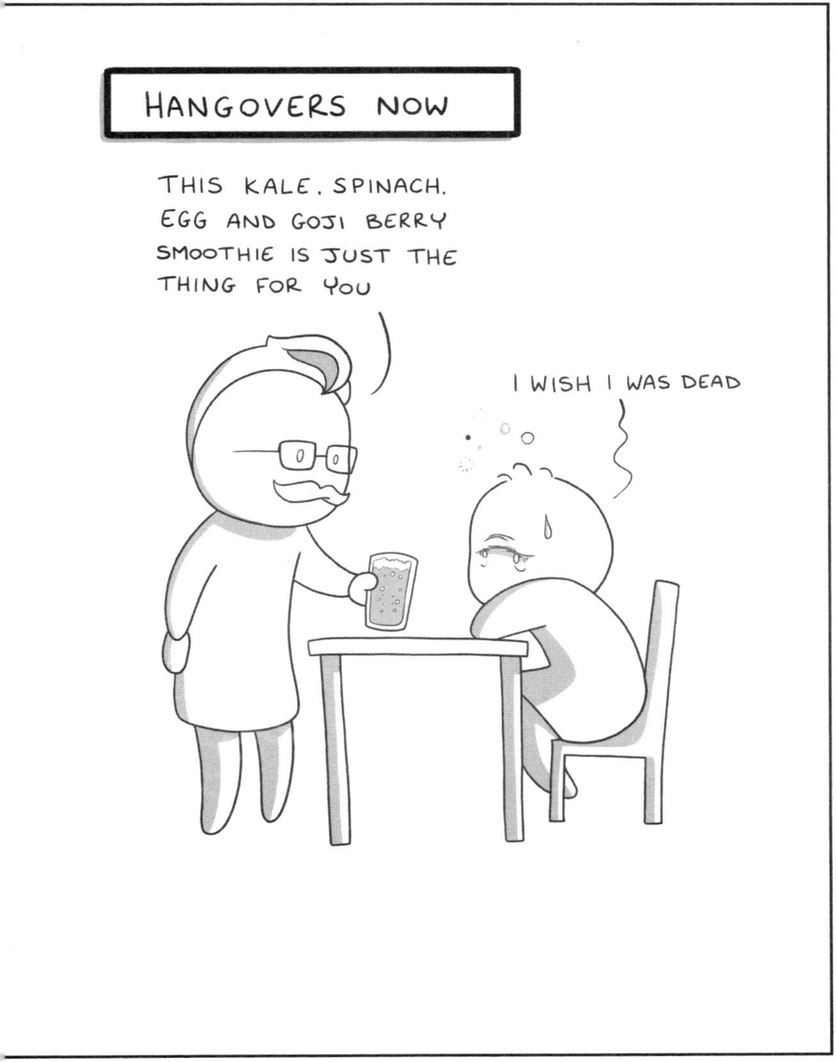
HANGOVERS NOW
THIS KALE, SPINACH, EGG AND GOJI BERRY SMOOTHIE IS JUST THE THING FOR YOU
I WISH I WAS DEAD

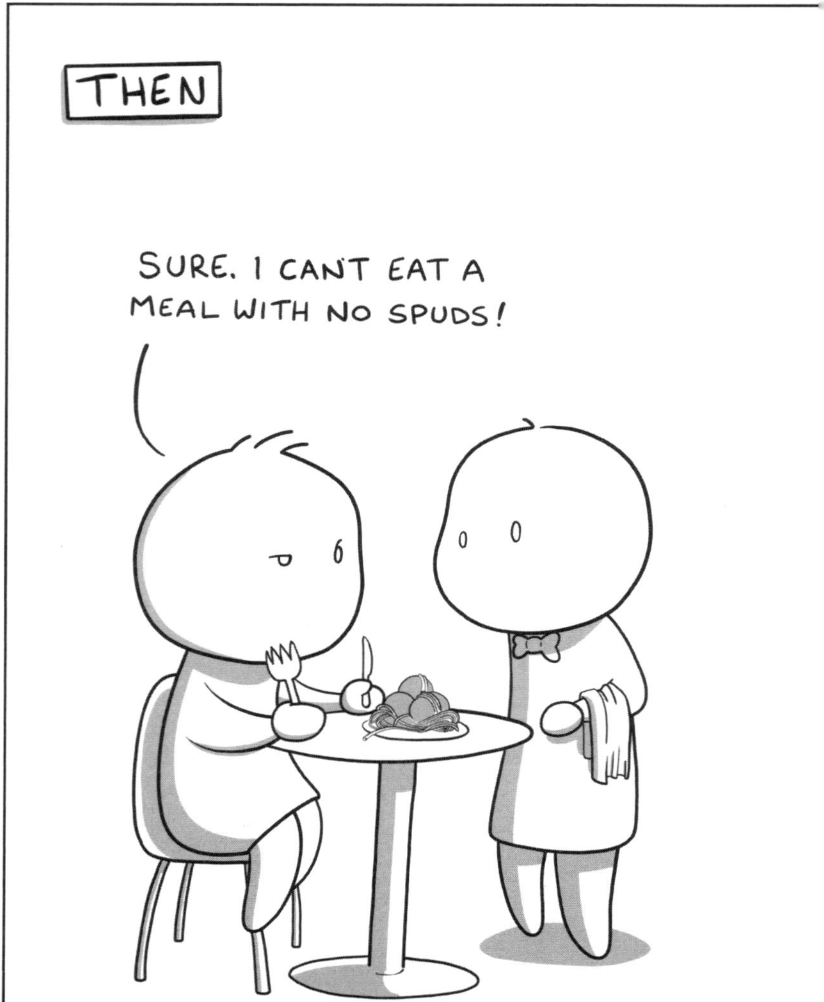
THEN
SURE. I CAN'T EAT A MEAL WITH NO SPUDS!

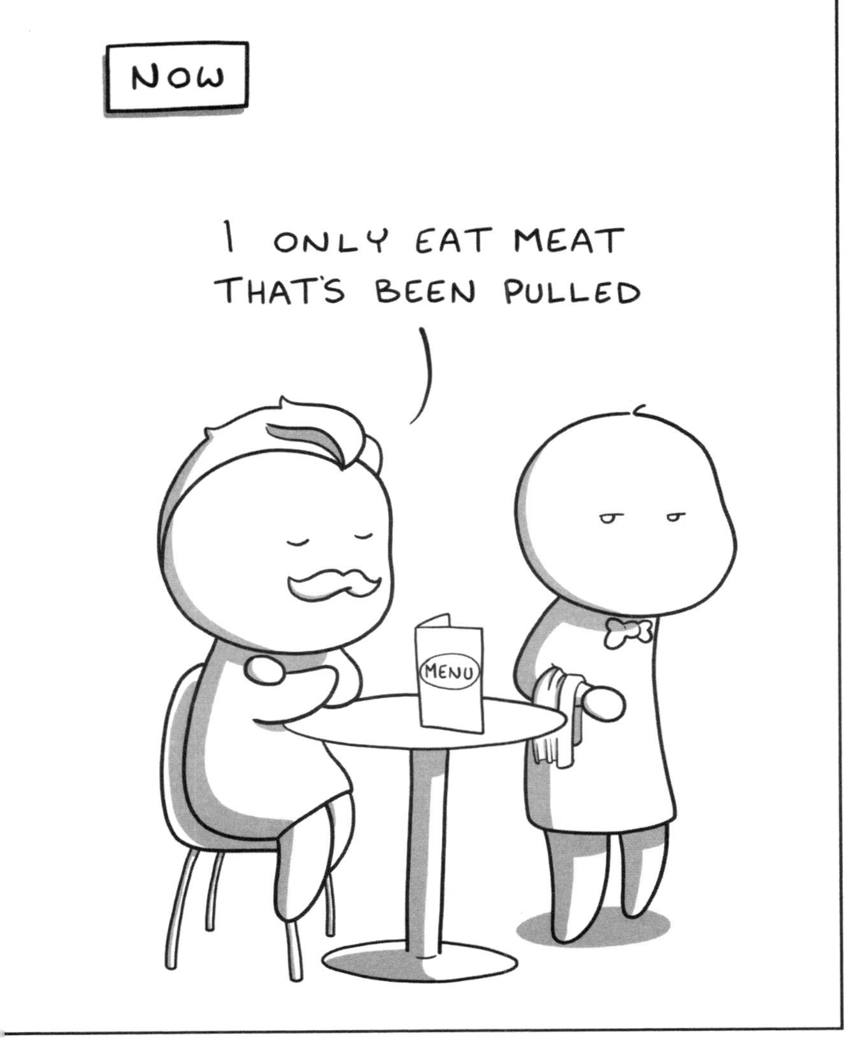
NOW
I ONLY EAT MEAT THAT'S BEEN PULLED
MENU

IN THE 80s A KID
COULD BUY SMOKES
BUT A WALNUT WHIP
WAS ADULTS ONLY

OVER 18s

ID REQUIRED

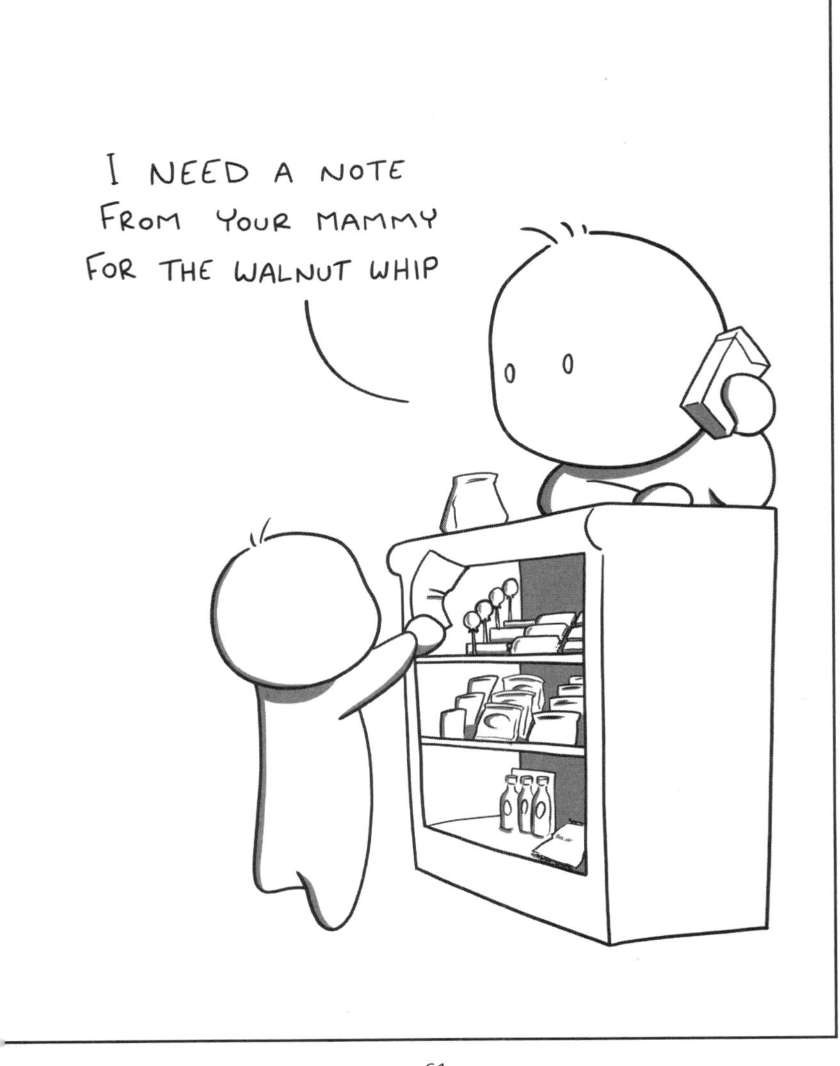
I NEED A NOTE FROM YOUR MAMMY FOR THE WALNUT WHIP

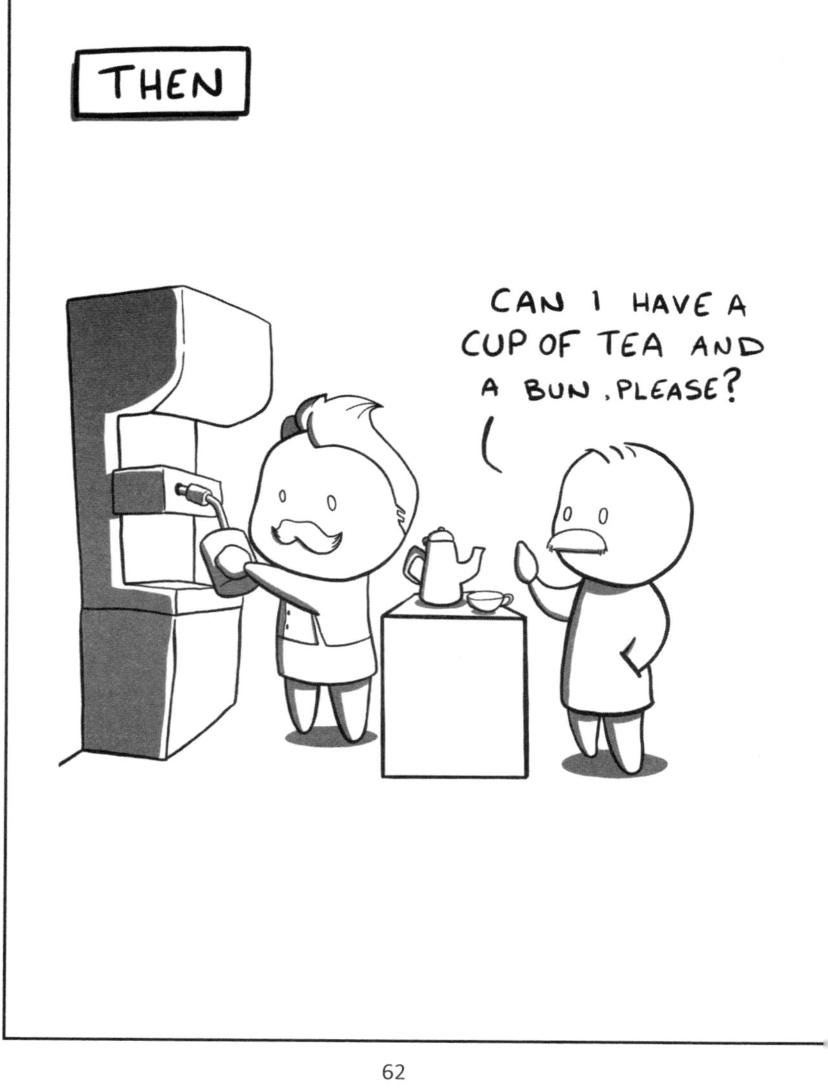
THEN
CAN I HAVE A CUP OF TEA AND A BUN, PLEASE?

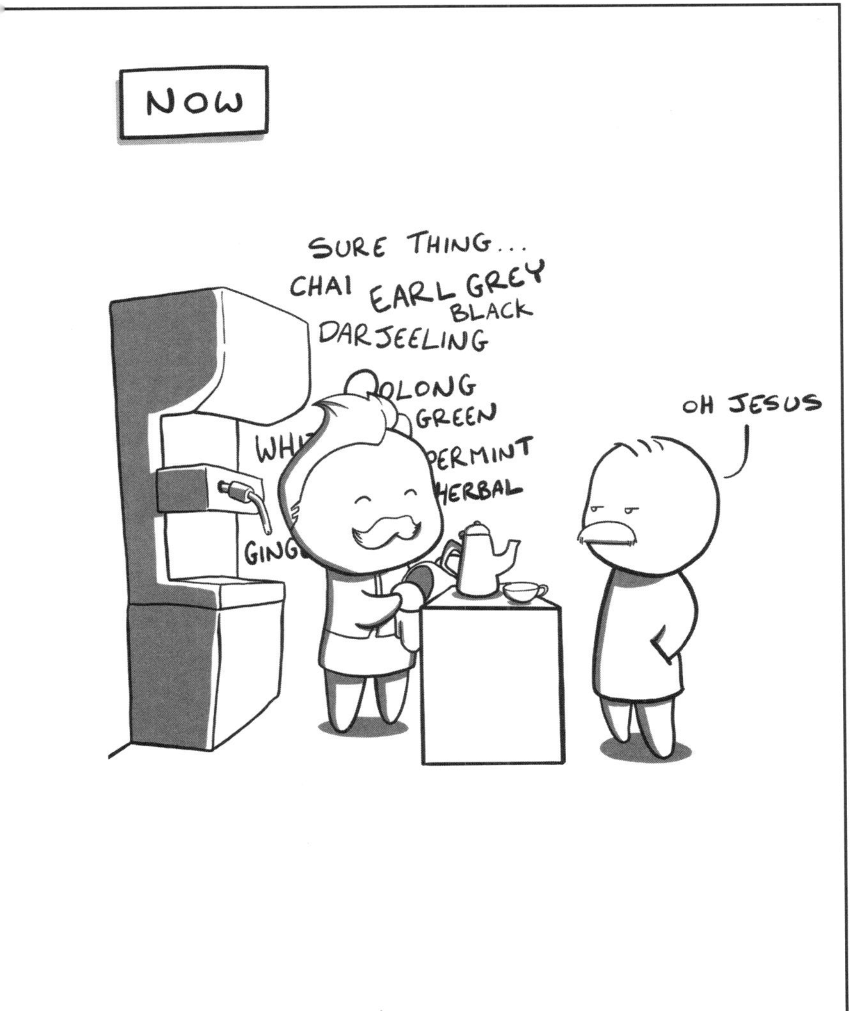
NOW
SURE THING...
CHAI
EARL GREY
BLACK
DARJEELING
OLONG
GREEN
WHI
PERMINT
HERBAL
GING
OH JESUS

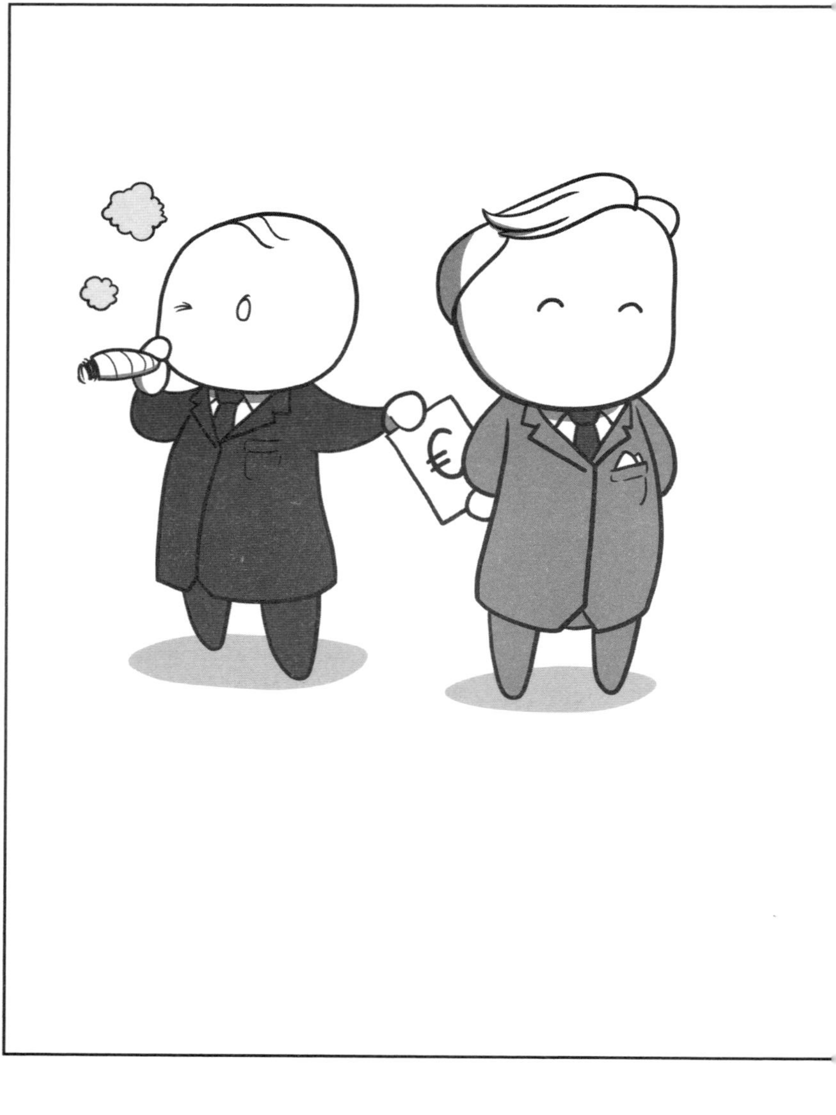

POLITICS AND LIFE IN IRELAND

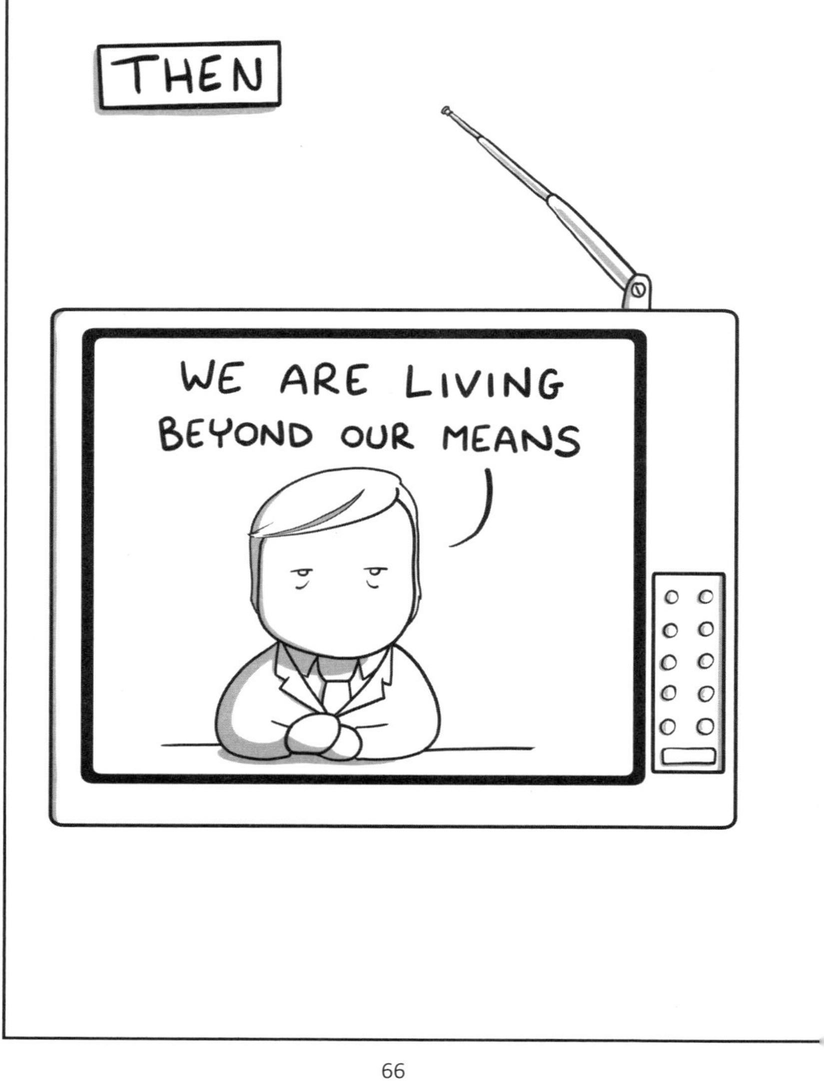
THEN
WE ARE LIVING BEYOND OUR MEANS

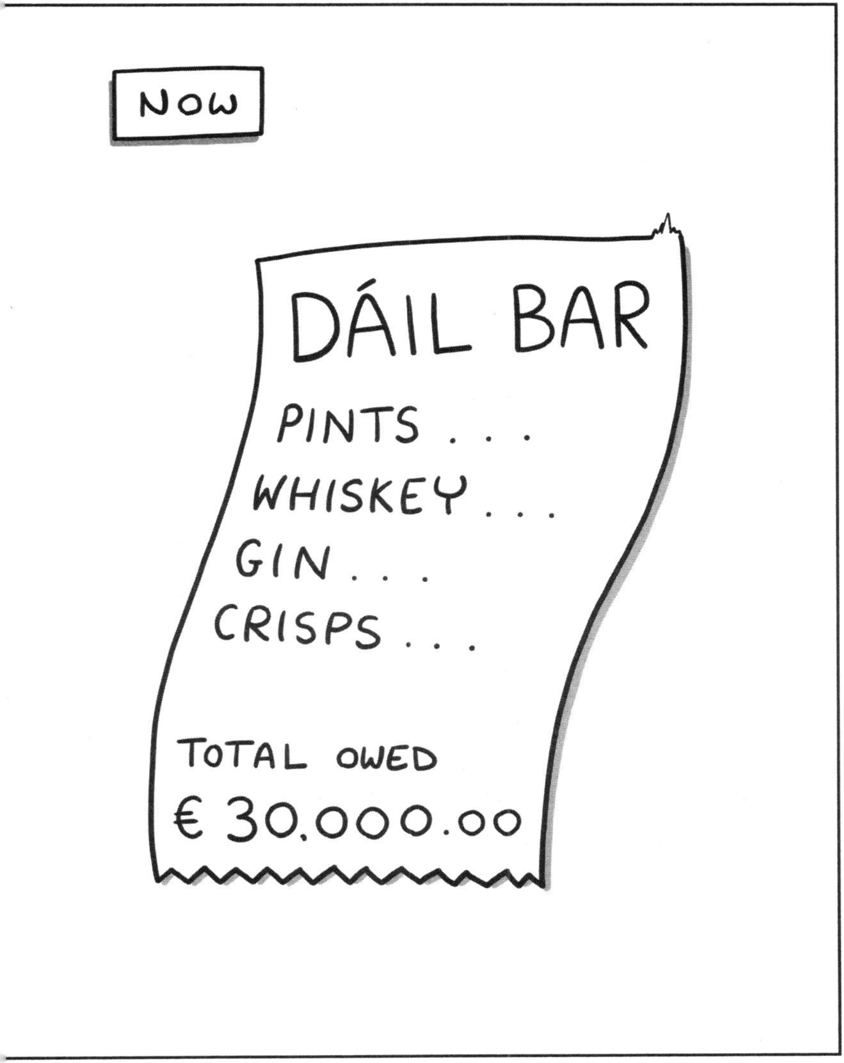
NOW
DÁIL BAR
PINTS . . .
WHISKEY . . .
GIN . . .
CRISPS . . .
TOTAL OWED
€ 30,000.00

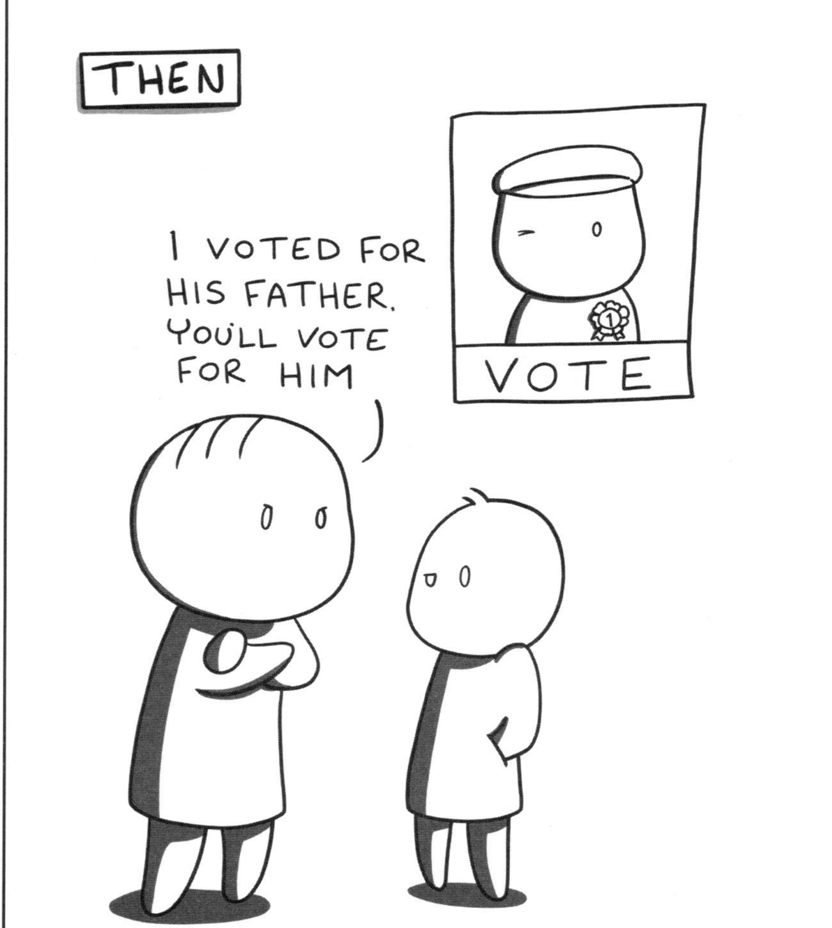
THEN
I VOTED FOR HIS FATHER. YOU'LL VOTE FOR HIM
VOTE

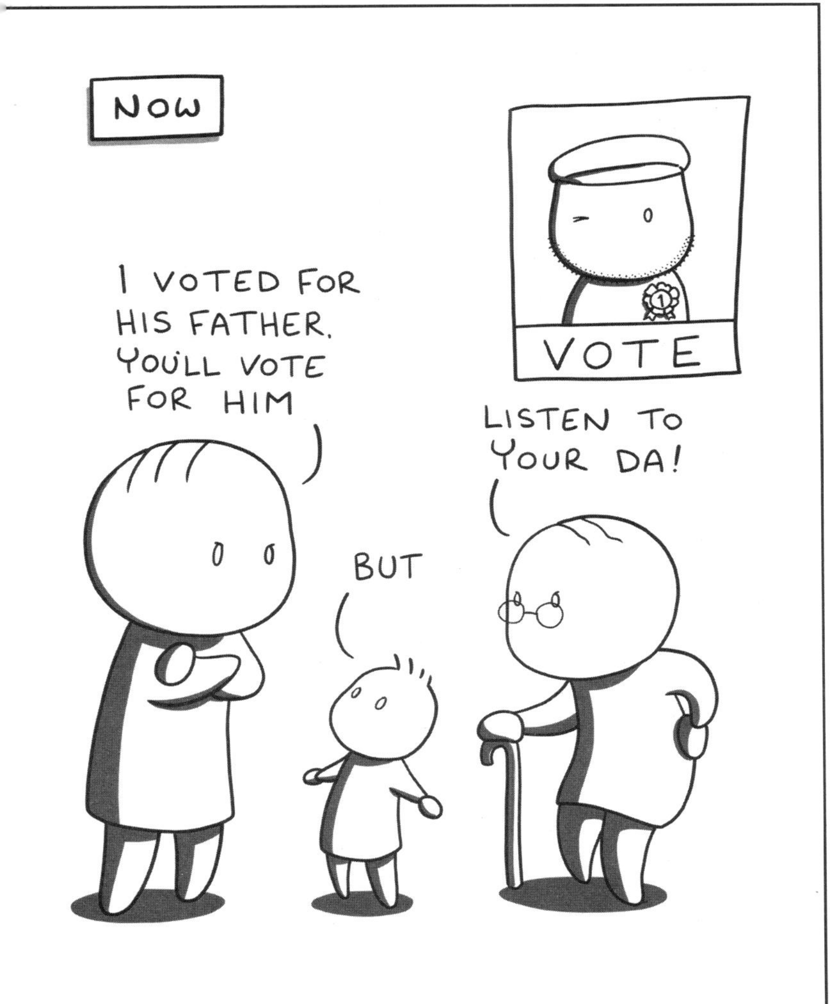
NOW
VOTE
I VOTED FOR HIS FATHER. YOU'LL VOTE FOR HIM
BUT
LISTEN TO YOUR DA!

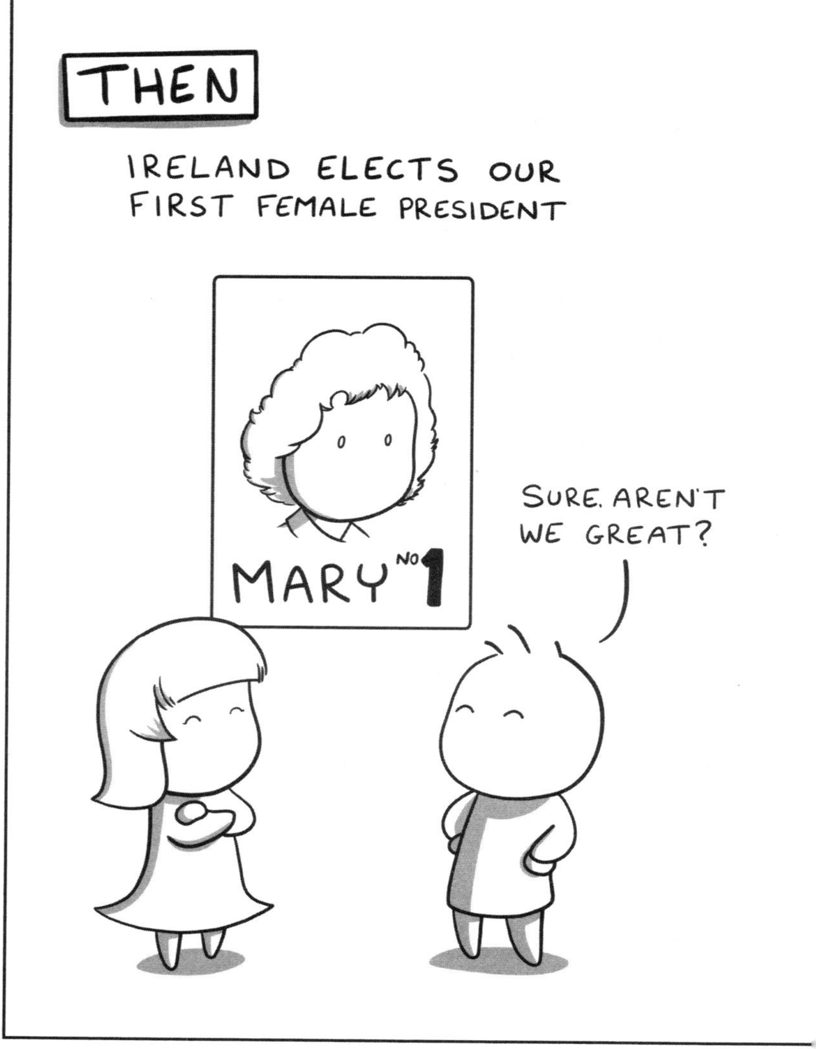
THEN
IRELAND ELECTS OUR FIRST FEMALE PRESIDENT
MARY NO 1
SURE. AREN'T WE GREAT?

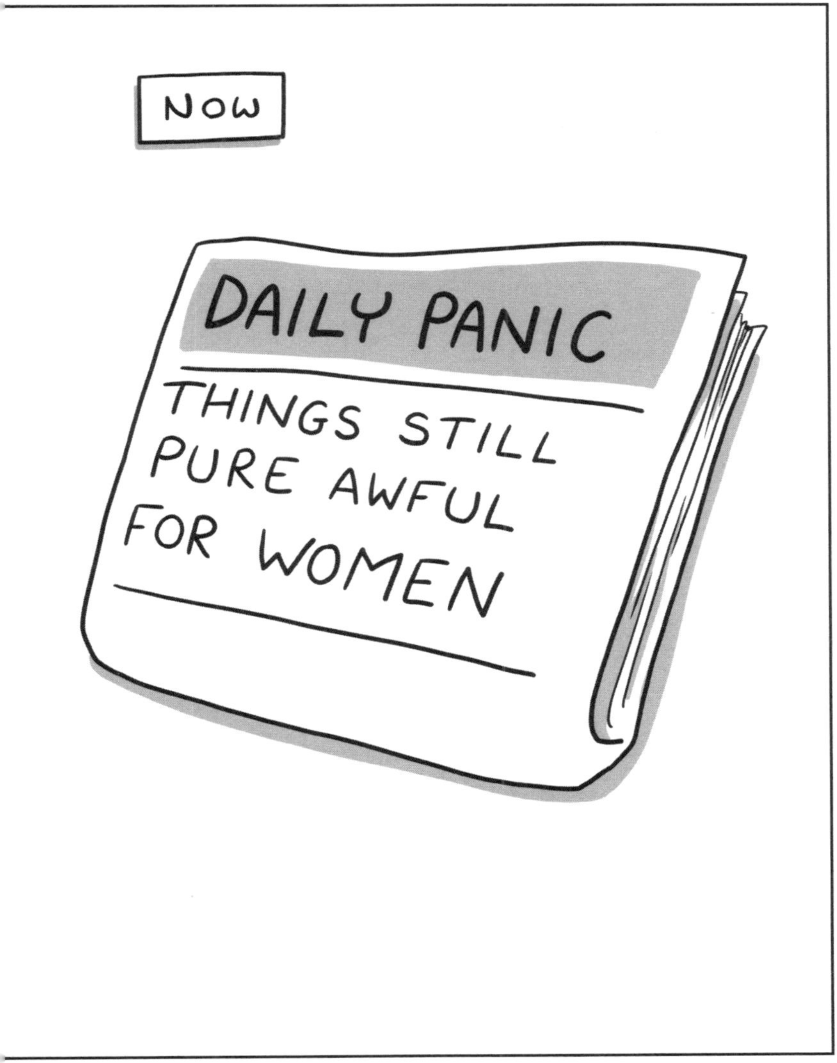
NOW
DAILY PANIC
THINGS STILL PURE AWFUL FOR WOMEN

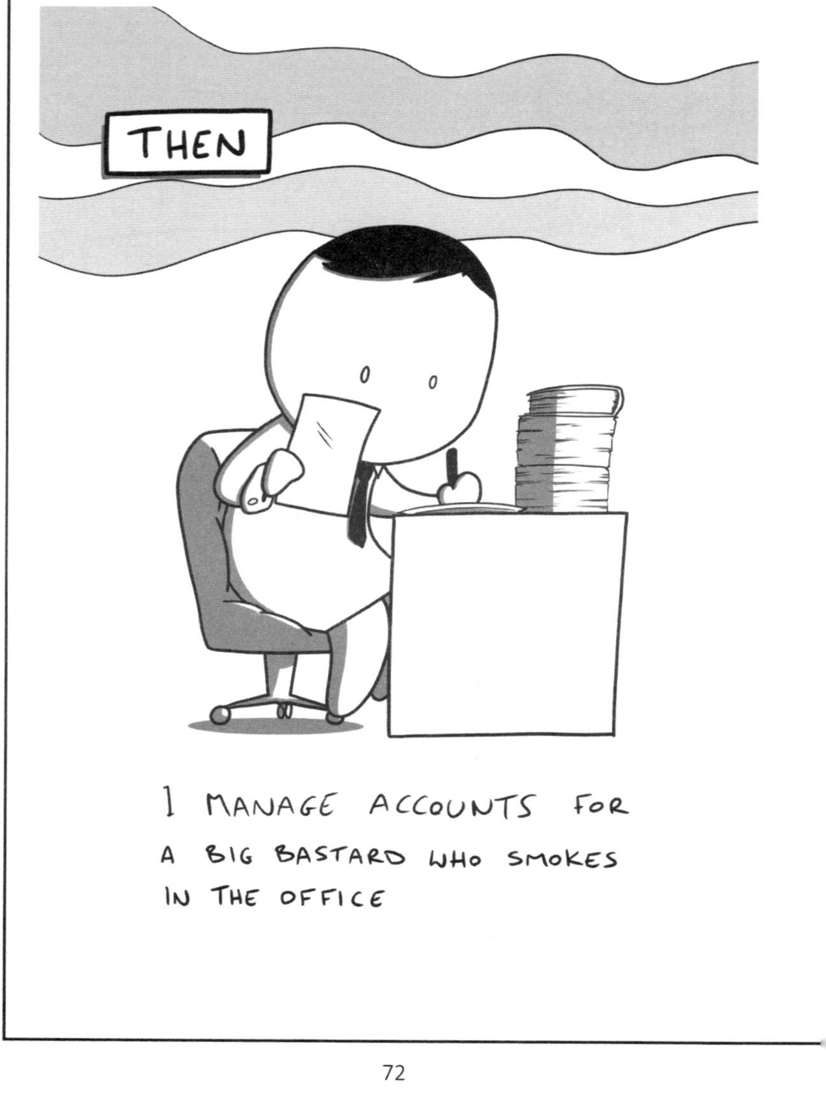
THEN
I MANAGE ACCOUNTS FOR
A BIG BASTARD WHO SMOKES
IN THE OFFICE

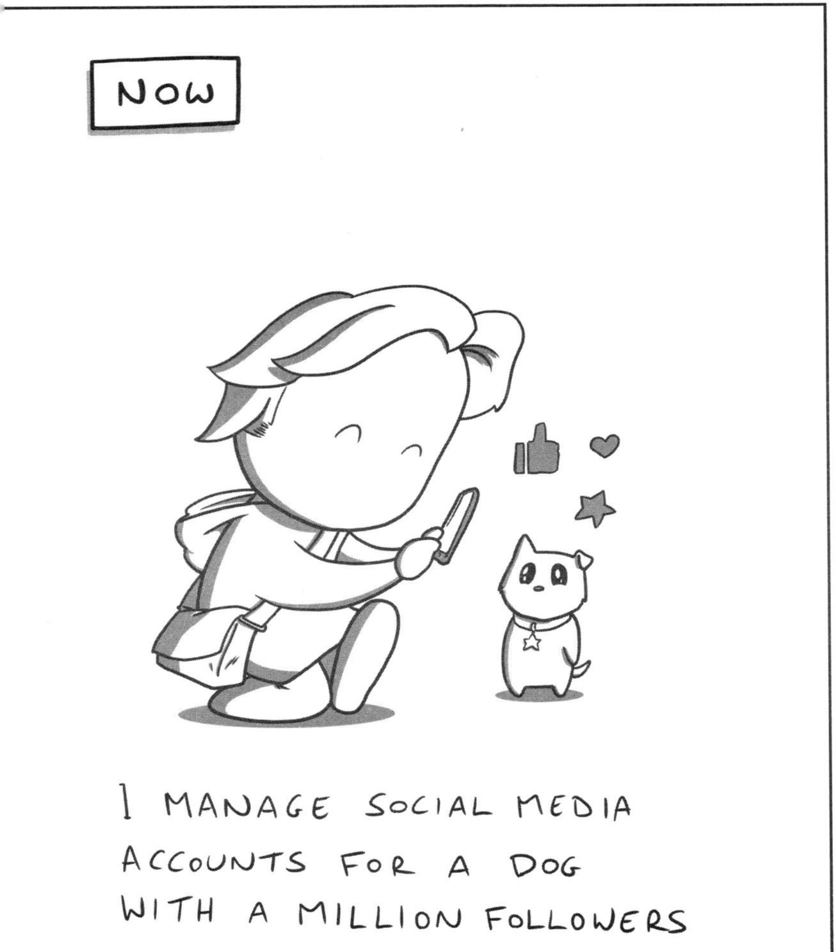
NOW
I MANAGE SOCIAL MEDIA ACCOUNTS FOR A DOG WITH A MILLION FOLLOWERS

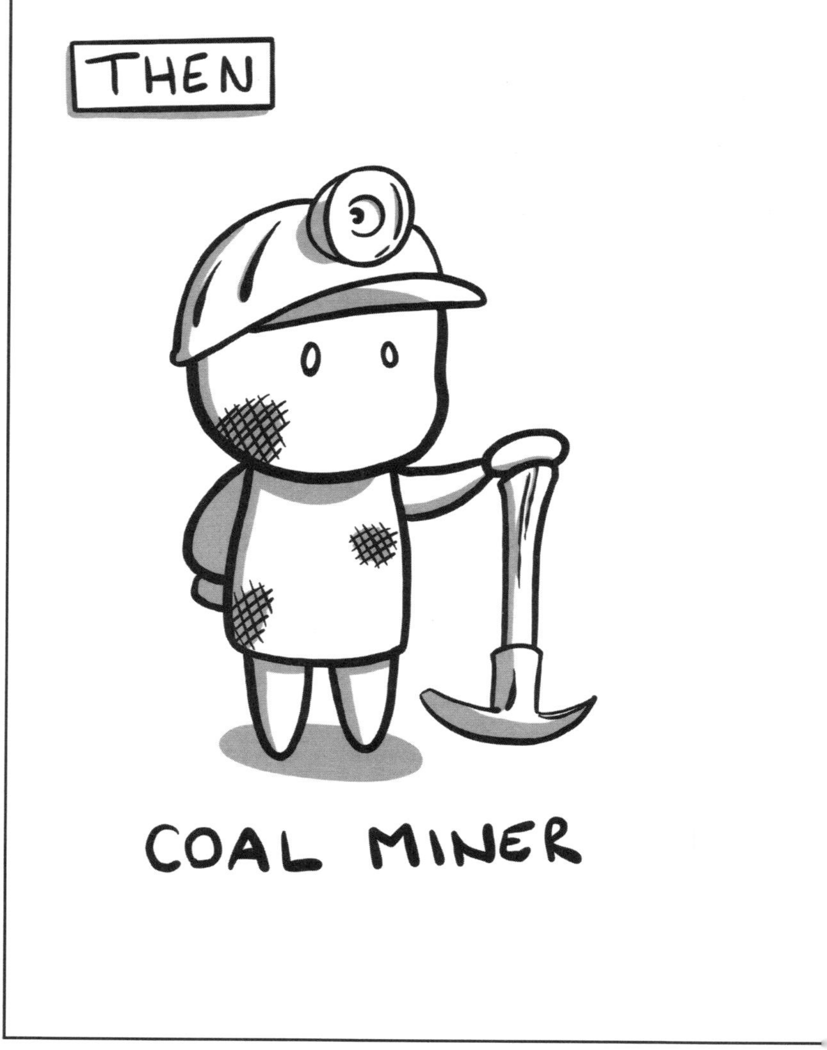
THEN
COAL MINER

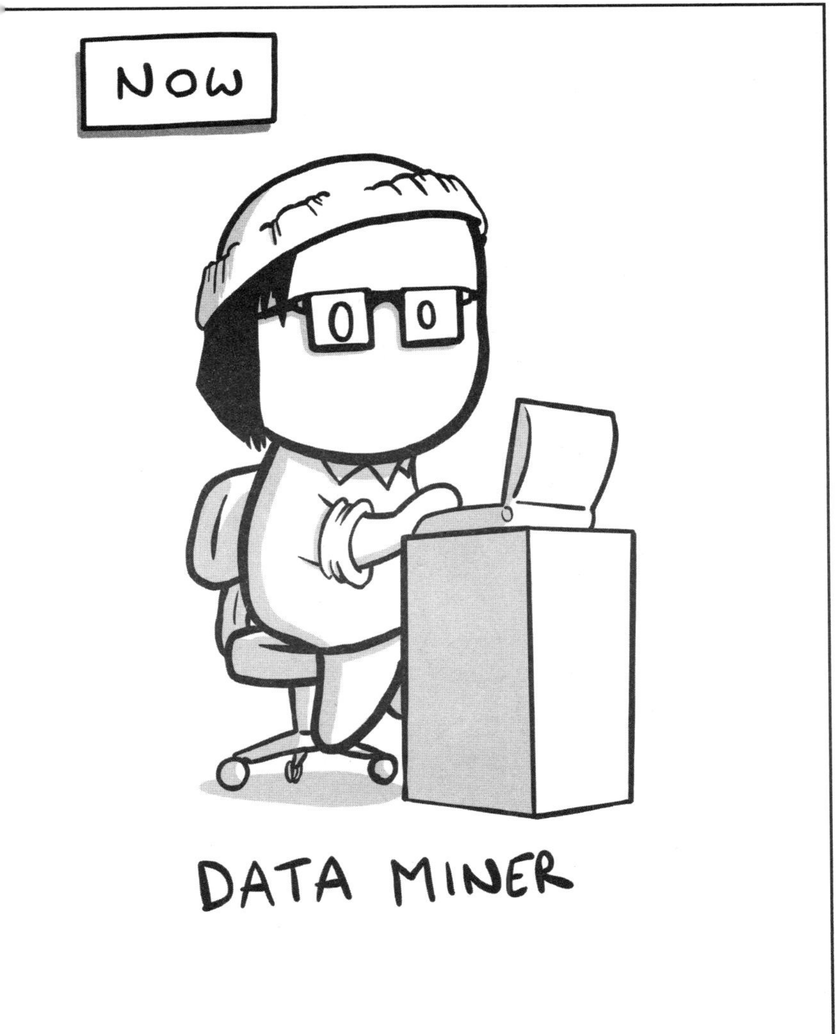
NOW
DATA MINER

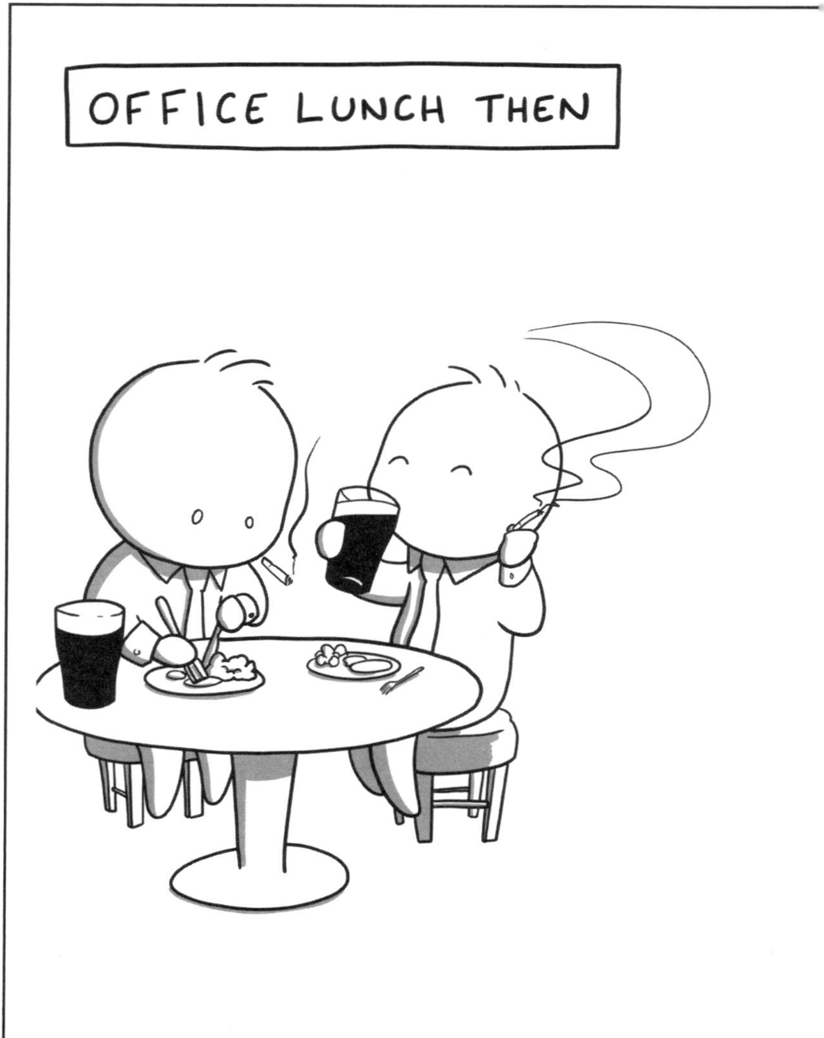
OFFICE LUNCH THEN

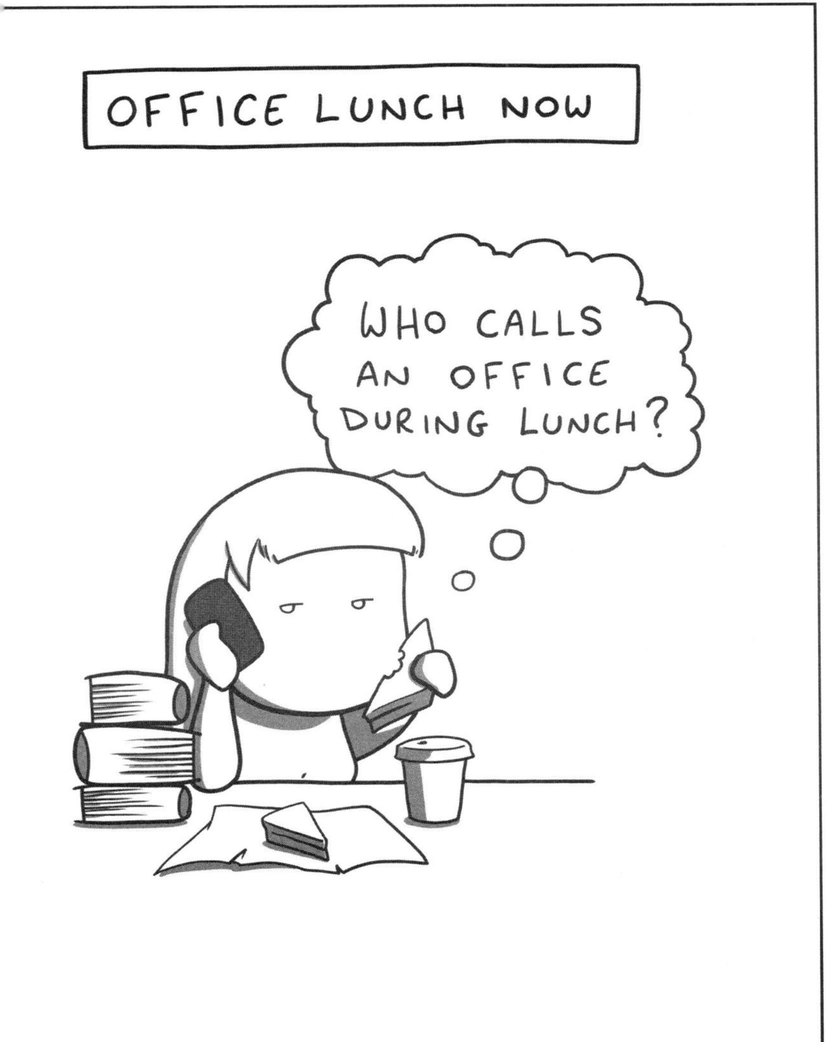
OFFICE LUNCH NOW
WHO CALLS AN OFFICE DURING LUNCH?

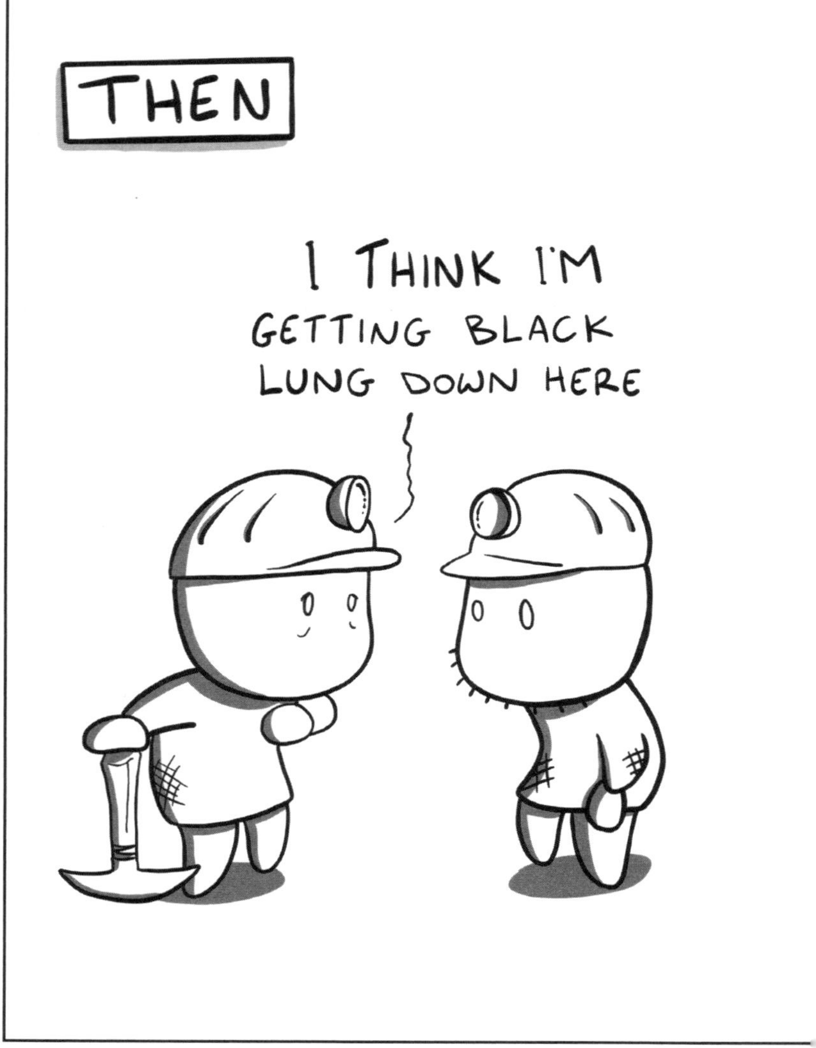
THEN
I THINK I'M GETTING BLACK LUNG DOWN HERE

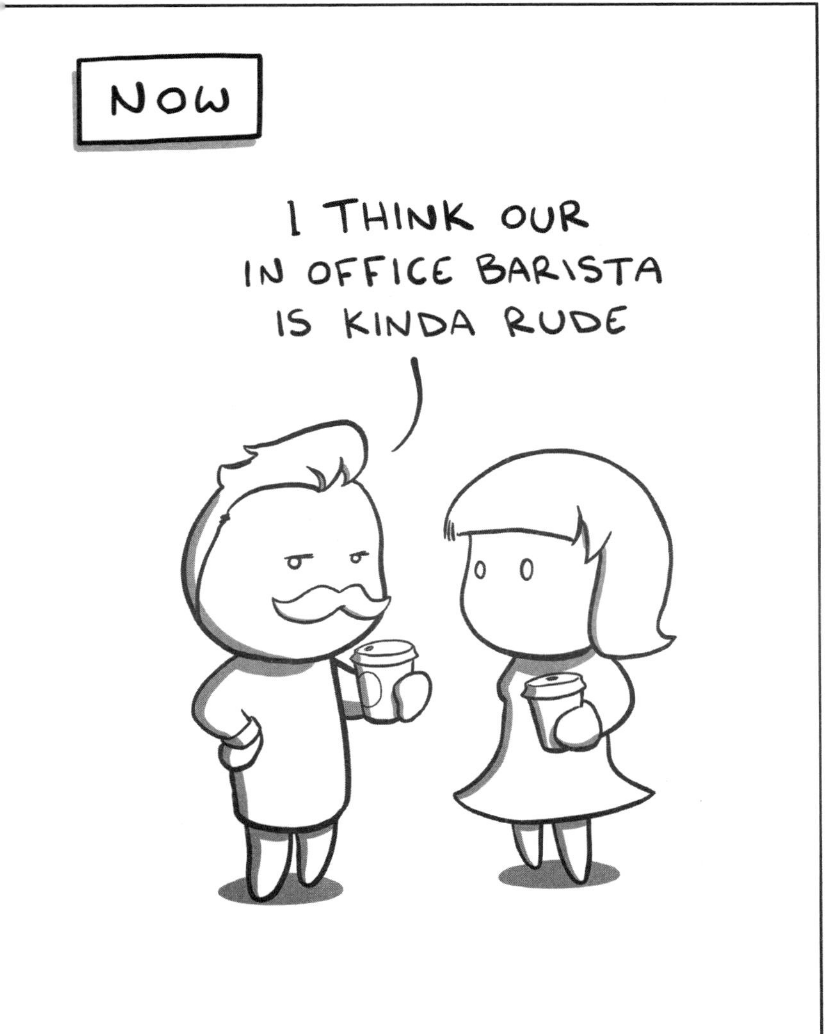
NOW
I THINK OUR
IN OFFICE BARISTA
IS KINDA RUDE

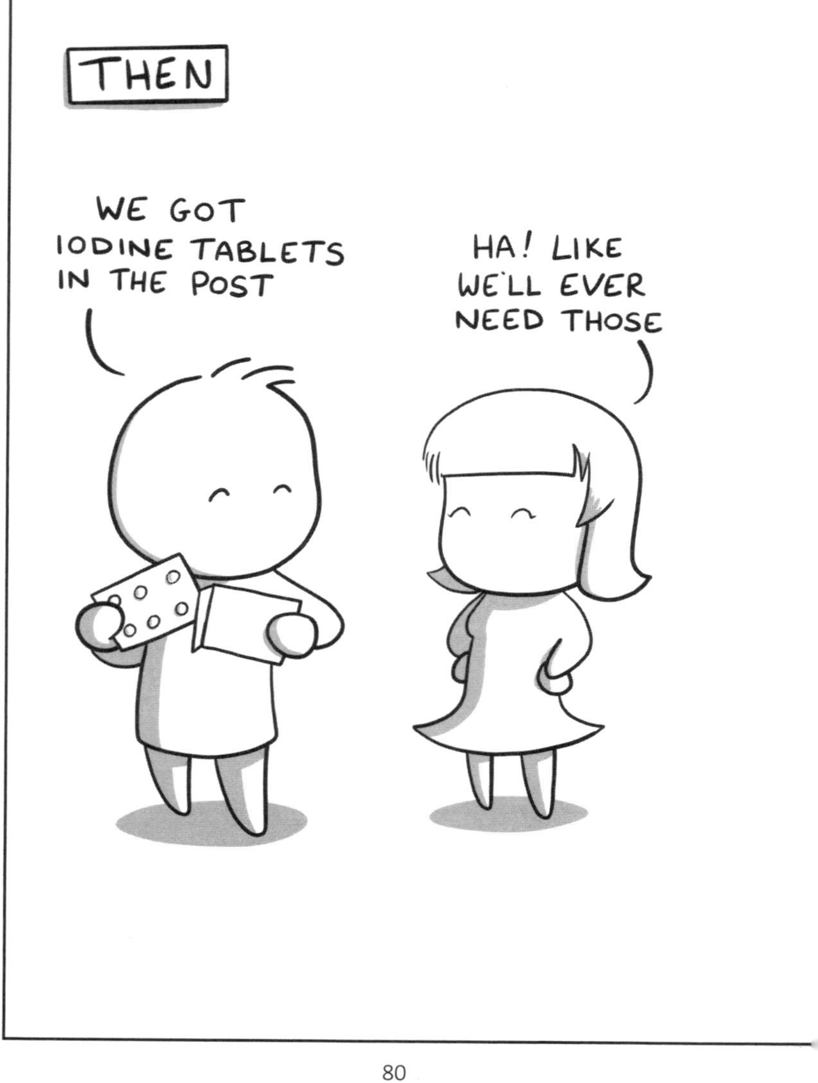
THEN
WE GOT IODINE TABLETS IN THE POST
HA! LIKE WE'LL EVER NEED THOSE

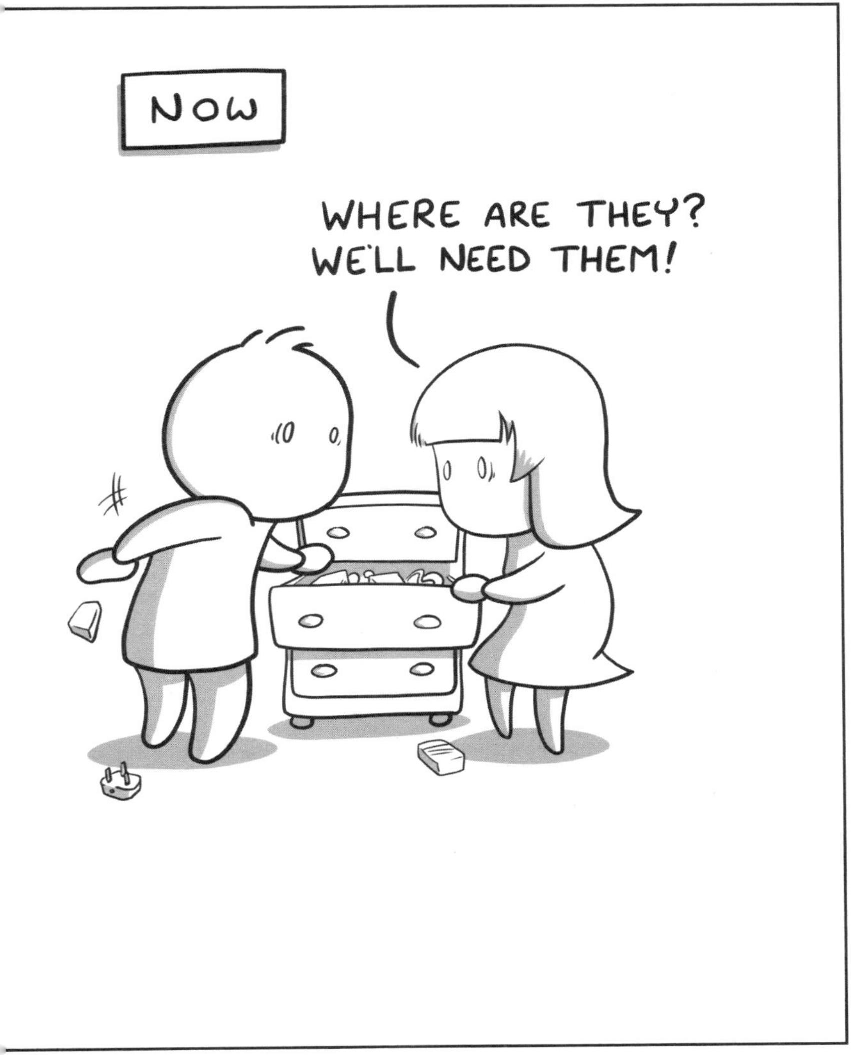
NOW
WHERE ARE THEY? WE'LL NEED THEM!

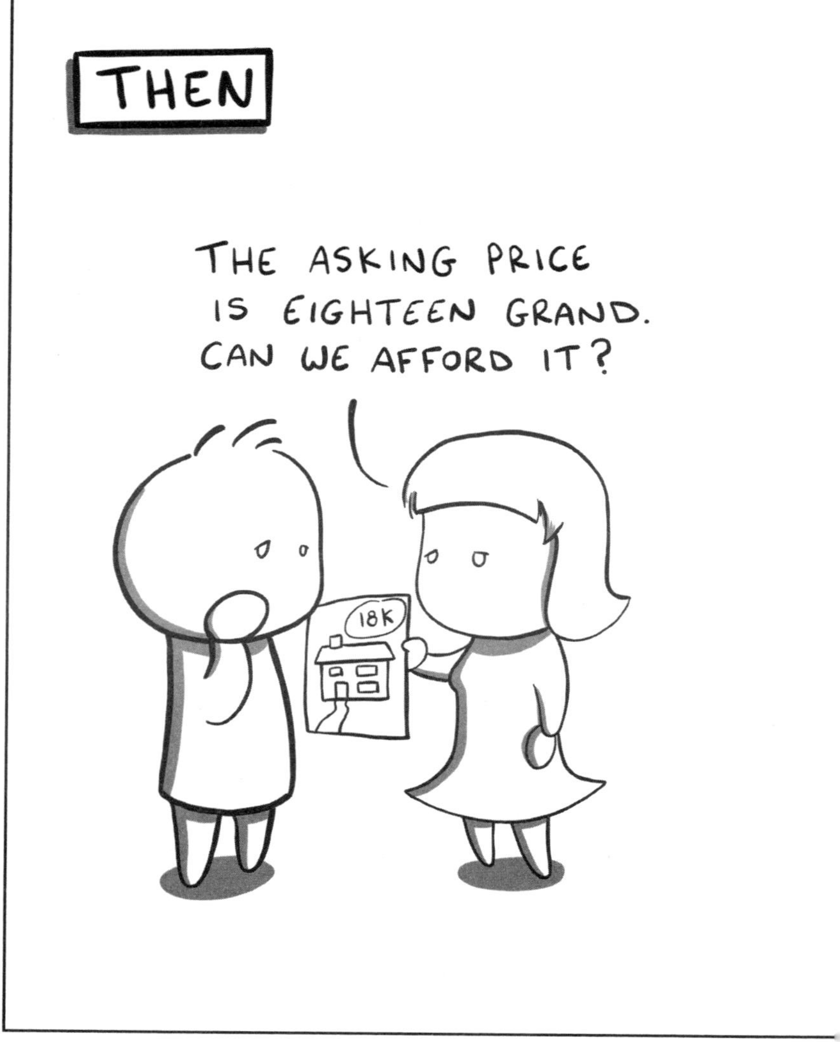
THEN
THE ASKING PRICE IS EIGHTEEN GRAND. CAN WE AFFORD IT?
18K

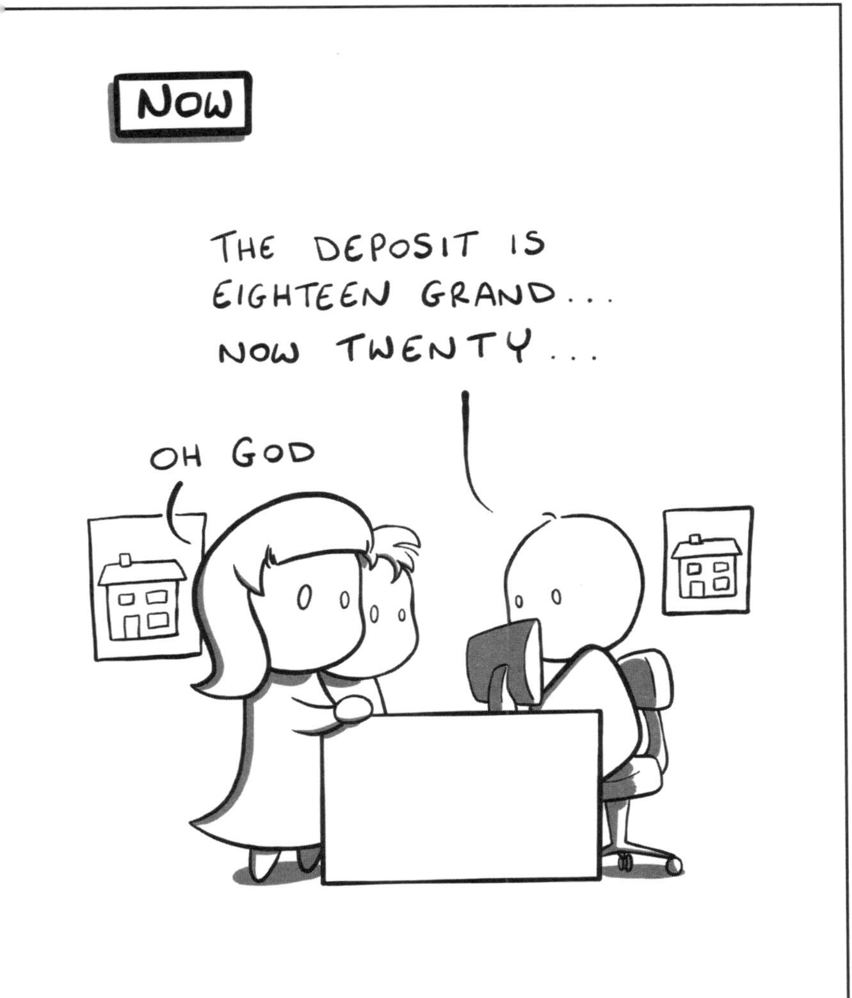
NOW
THE DEPOSIT IS EIGHTEEN GRAND... NOW TWENTY...
OH GOD

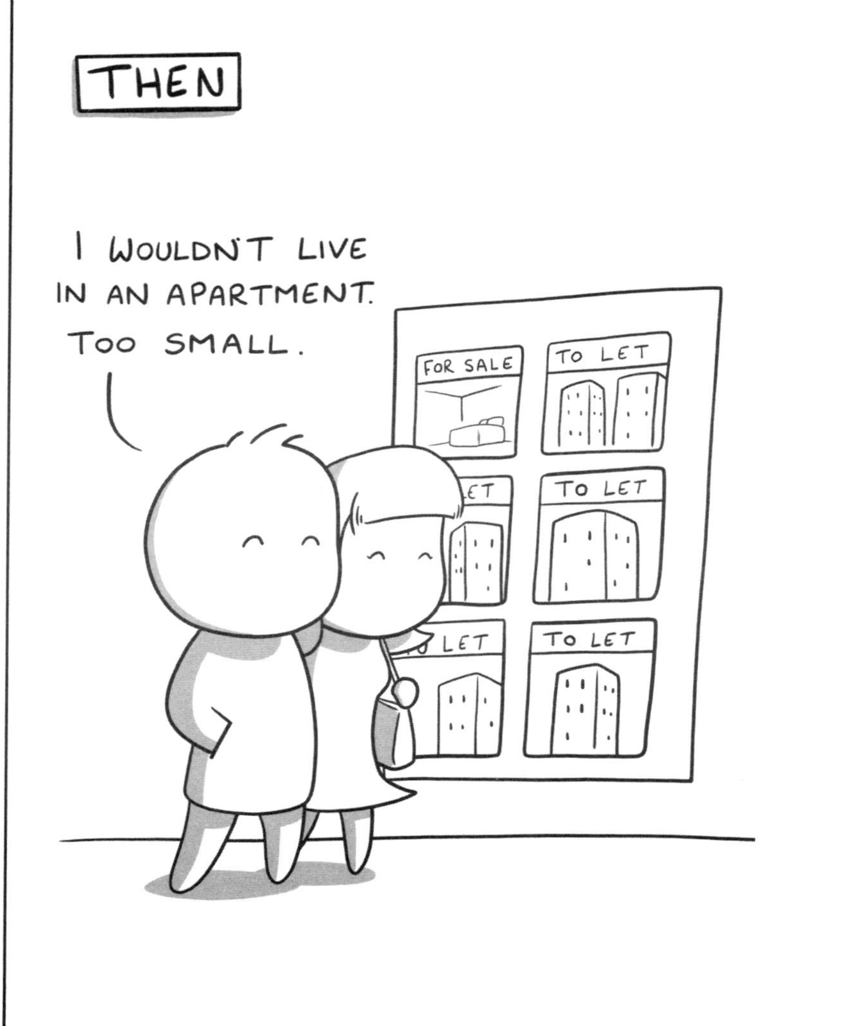
THEN
I WOULDN'T LIVE IN AN APARTMENT. TOO SMALL.
FOR SALE
TO LET
TO LET
TO LET

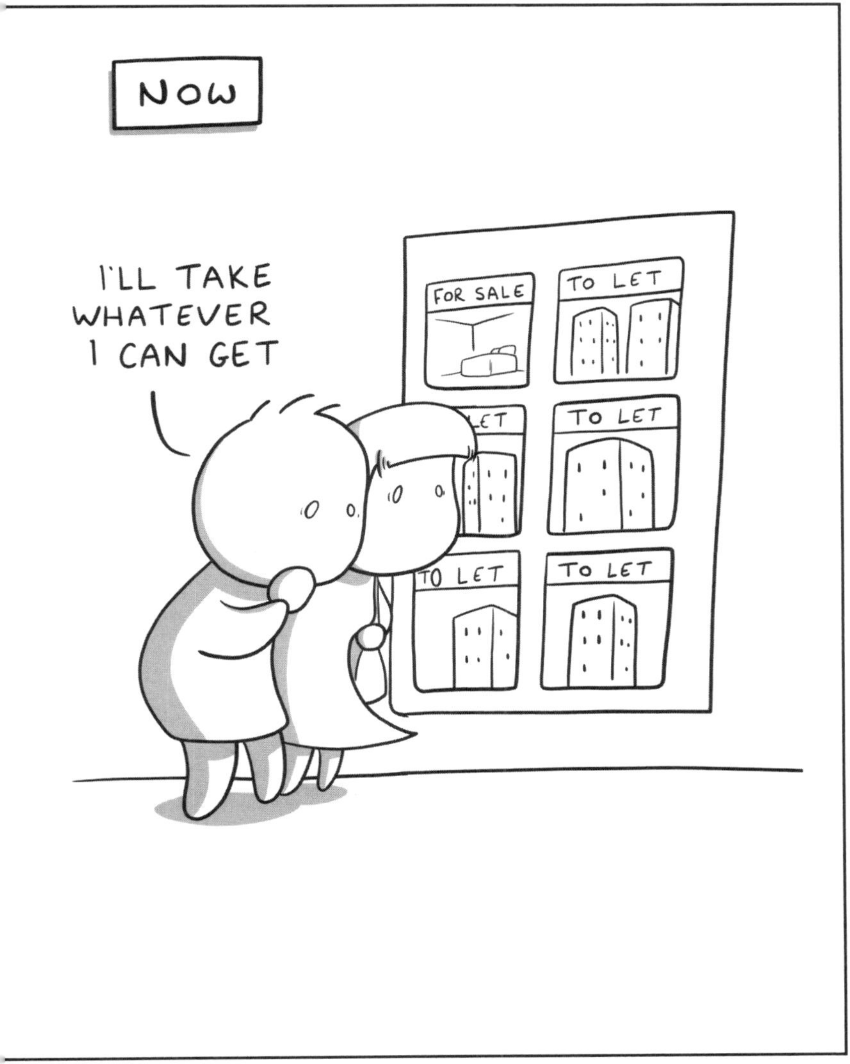
NOW
I'LL TAKE WHATEVER I CAN GET
FOR SALE
TO LET
TO LET
TO LET
TO LET

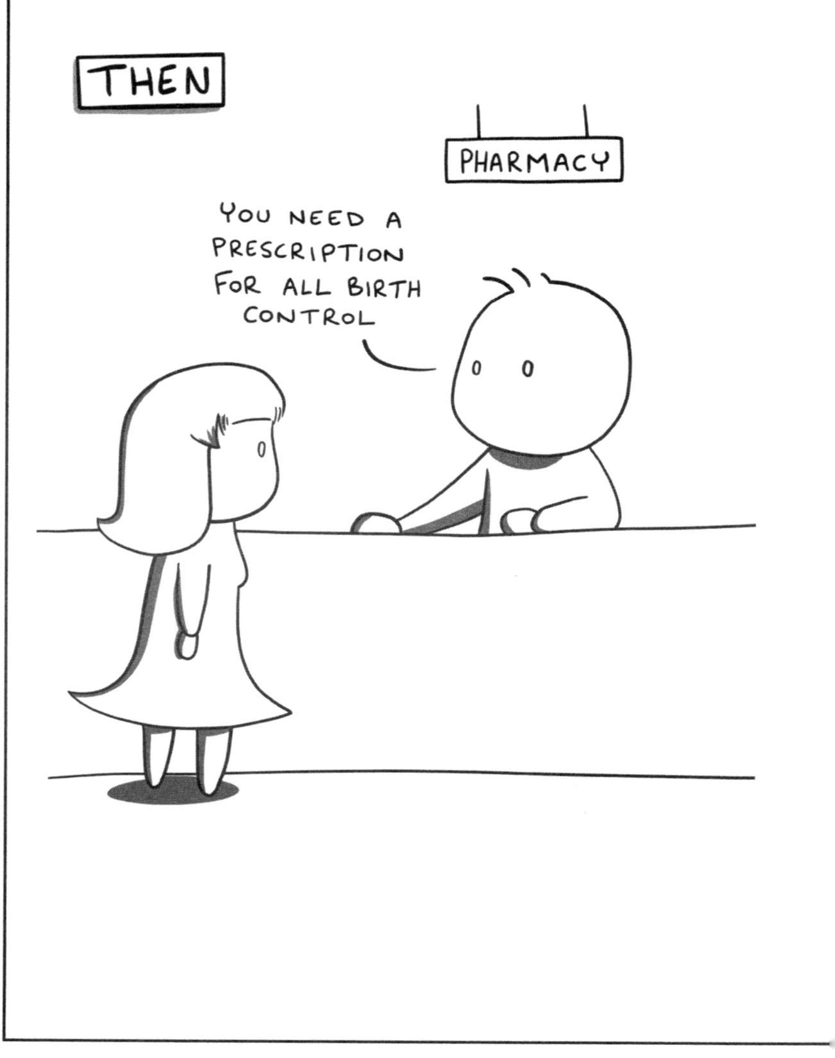
THEN
PHARMACY
YOU NEED A PRESCRIPTION FOR ALL BIRTH CONTROL

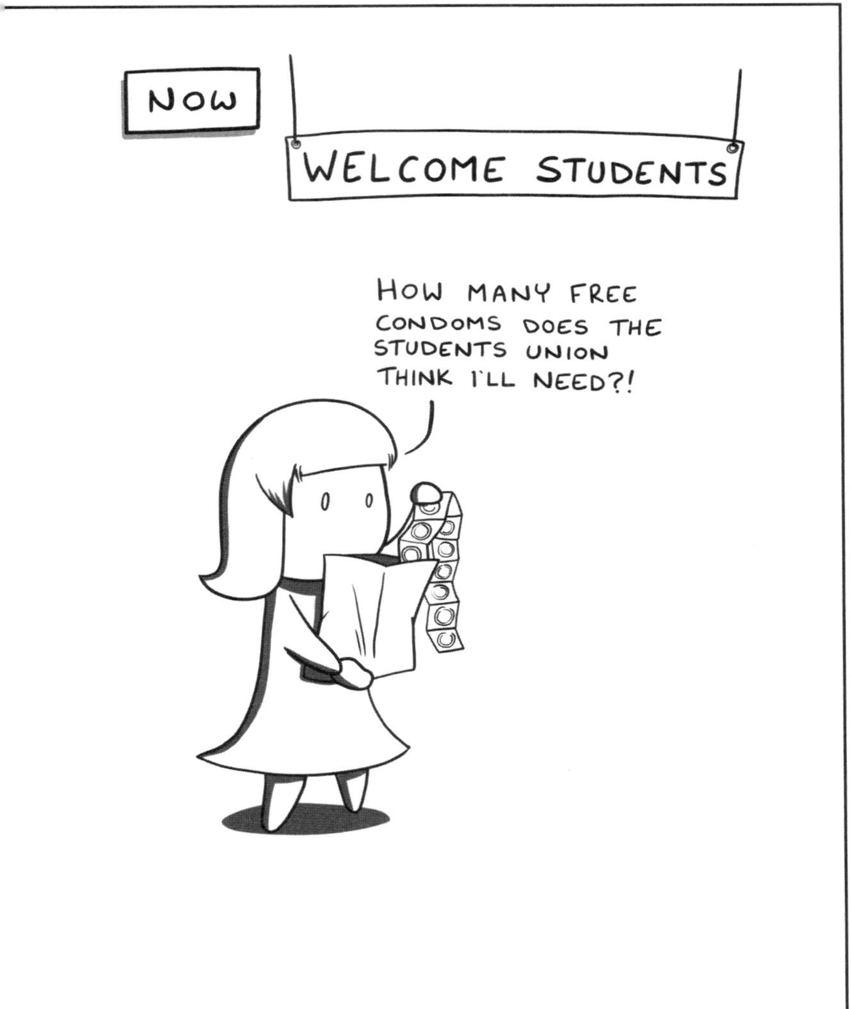
NOW
WELCOME STUDENTS
HOW MANY FREE CONDOMS DOES THE STUDENTS UNION THINK I'LL NEED?!

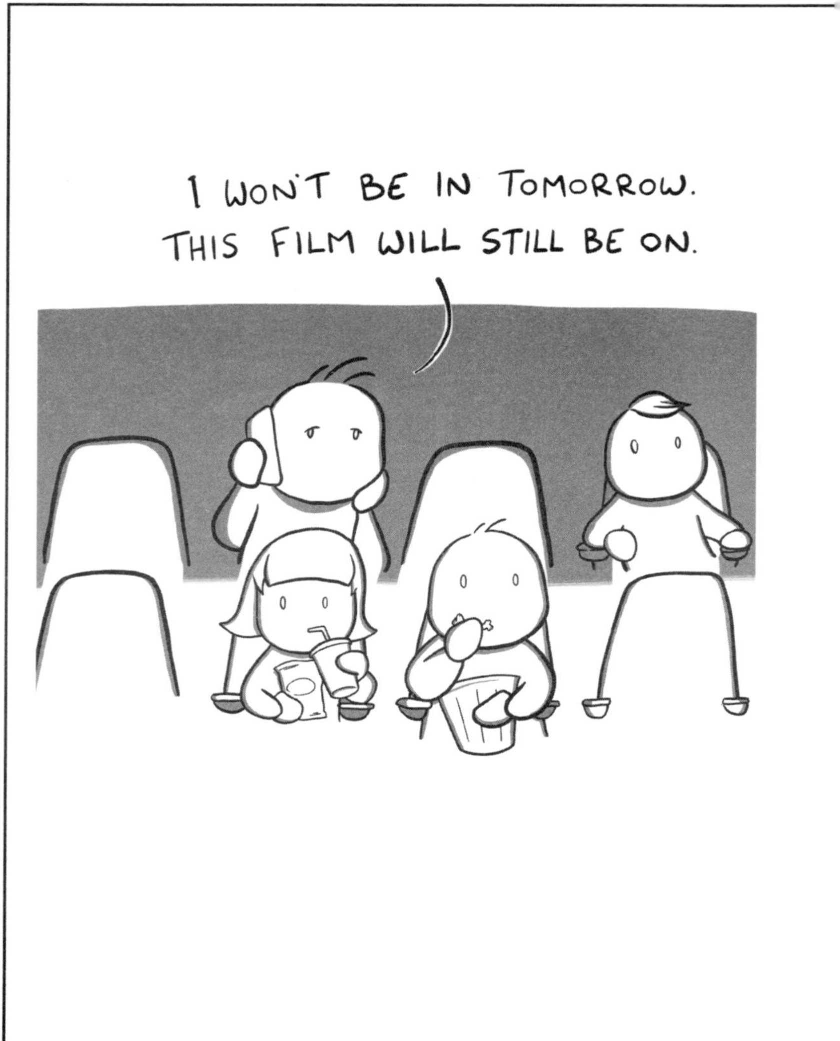
I WON'T BE IN TOMORROW.
THIS FILM WILL STILL BE ON.

ENTERTAINMENT

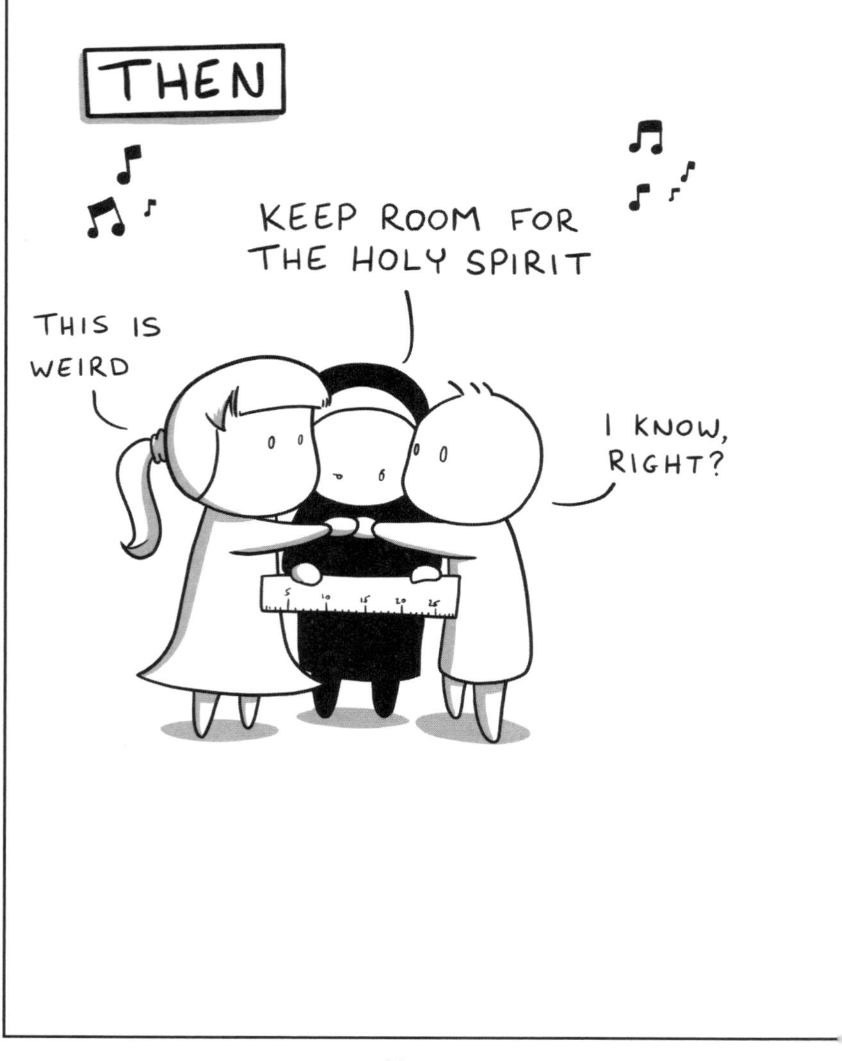
THEN
THIS IS WEIRD
KEEP ROOM FOR THE HOLY SPIRIT
I KNOW, RIGHT?

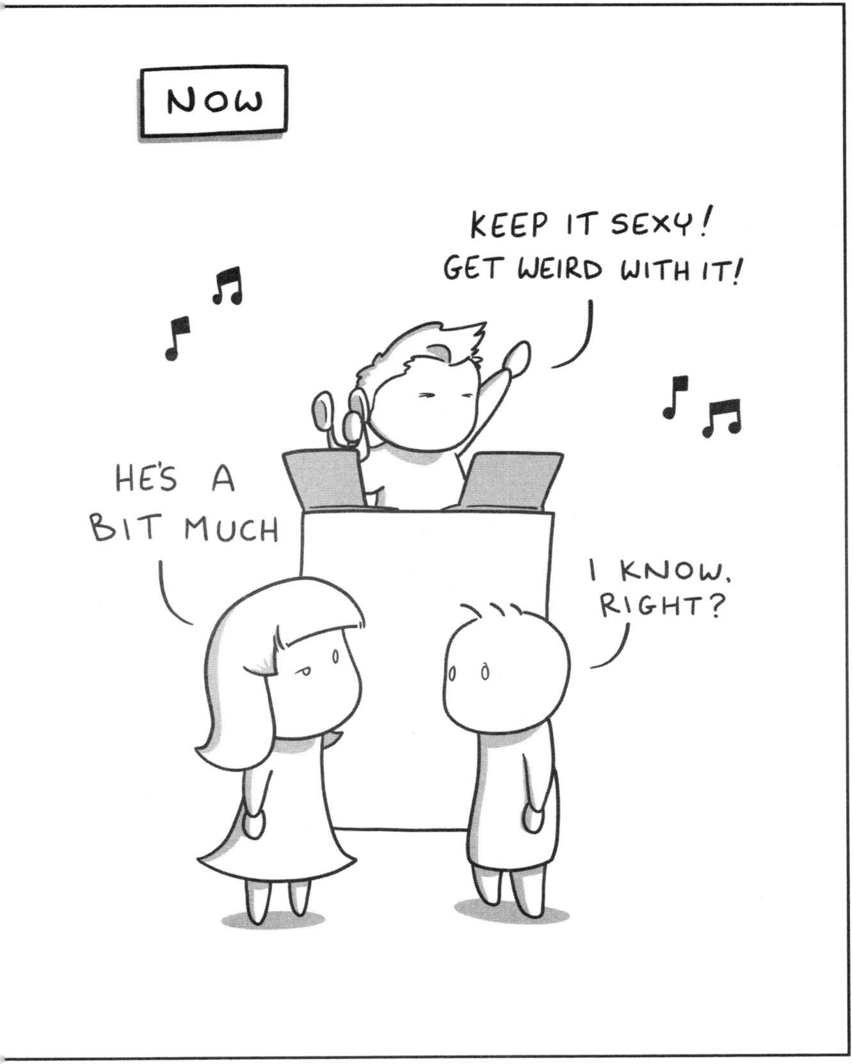
NOW
KEEP IT SEXY! GET WEIRD WITH IT!
HE'S A BIT MUCH
I KNOW, RIGHT?

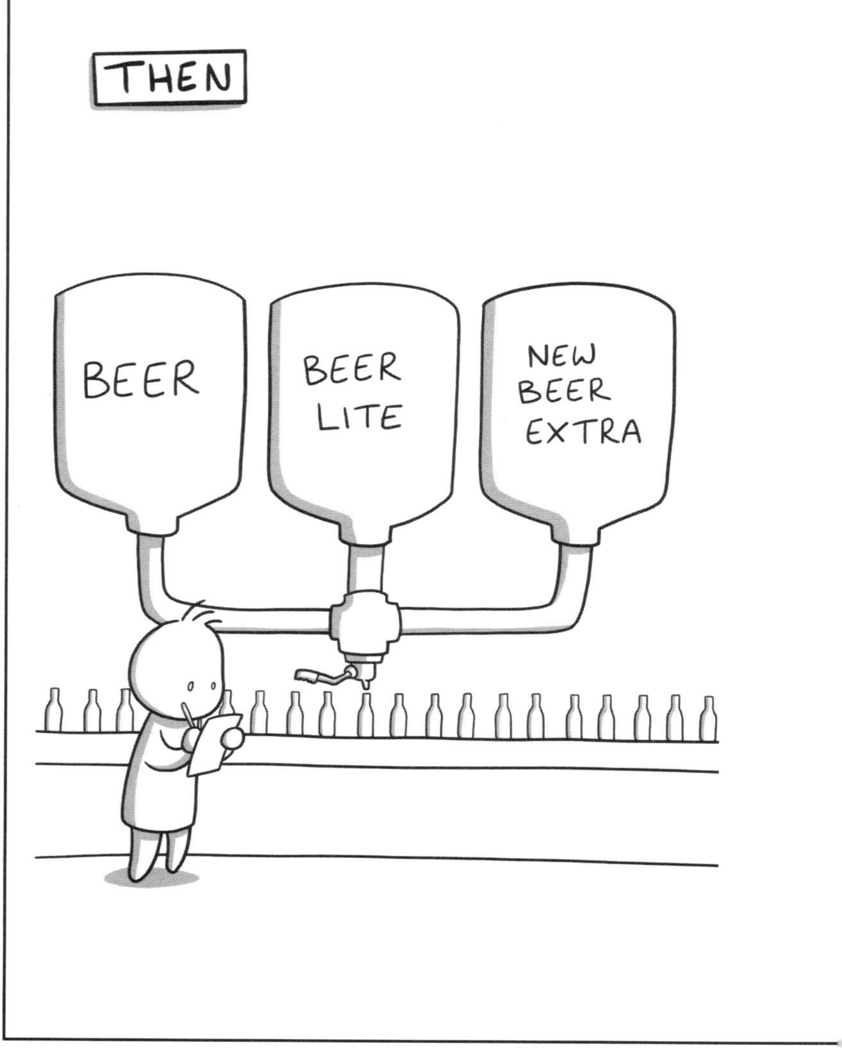
THEN
BEER
BEER
LITE
NEW
BEER
EXTRA

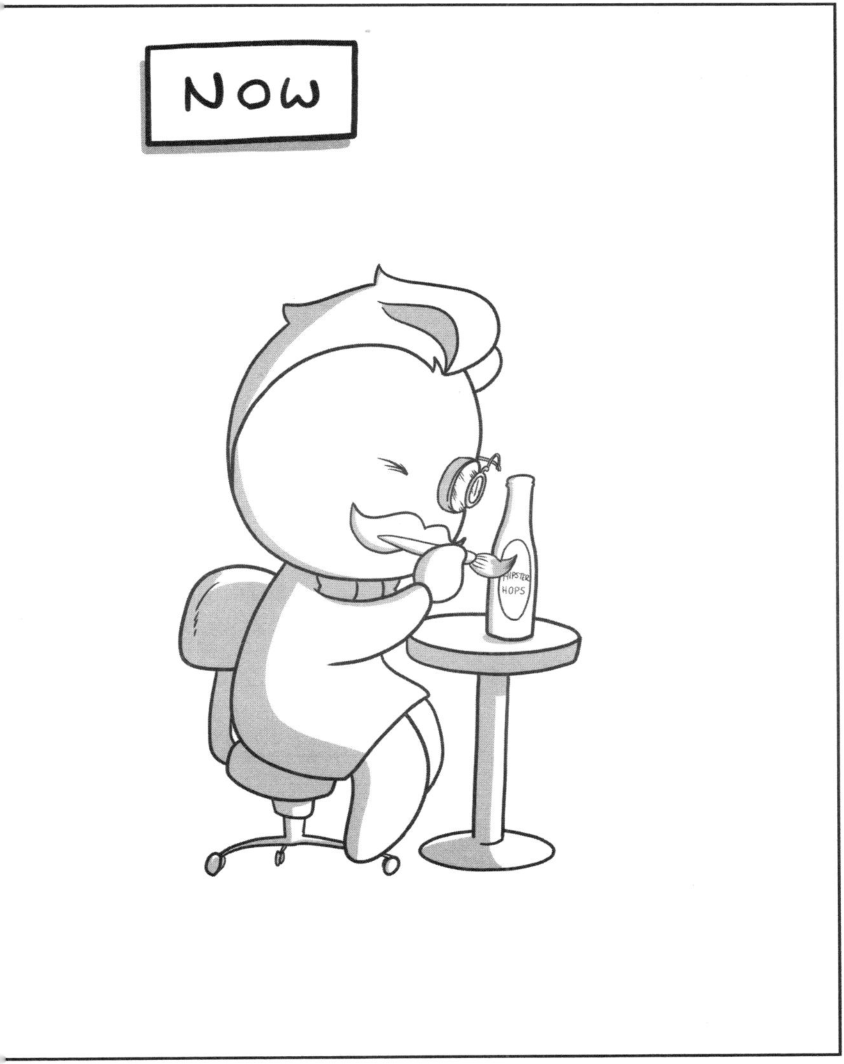
NOW
HIPSTER
HOPS

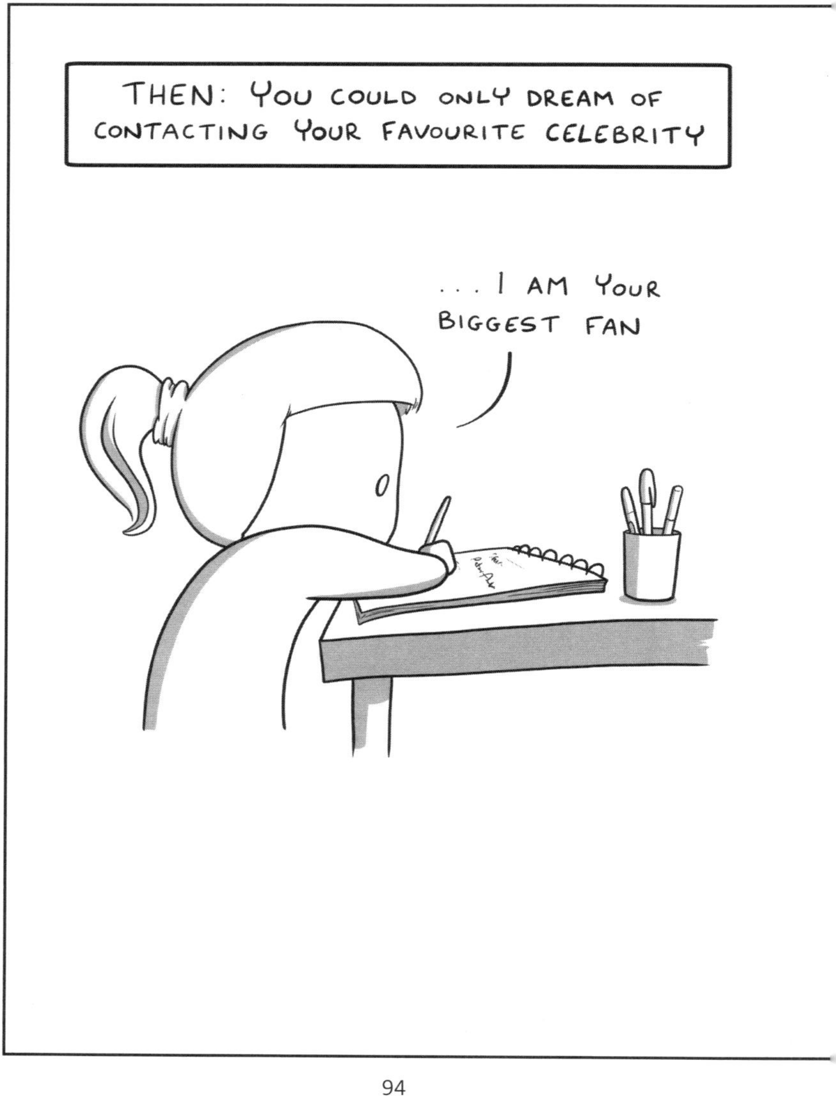
THEN: YOU COULD ONLY DREAM OF CONTACTING YOUR FAVOURITE CELEBRITY
...I AM YOUR BIGGEST FAN

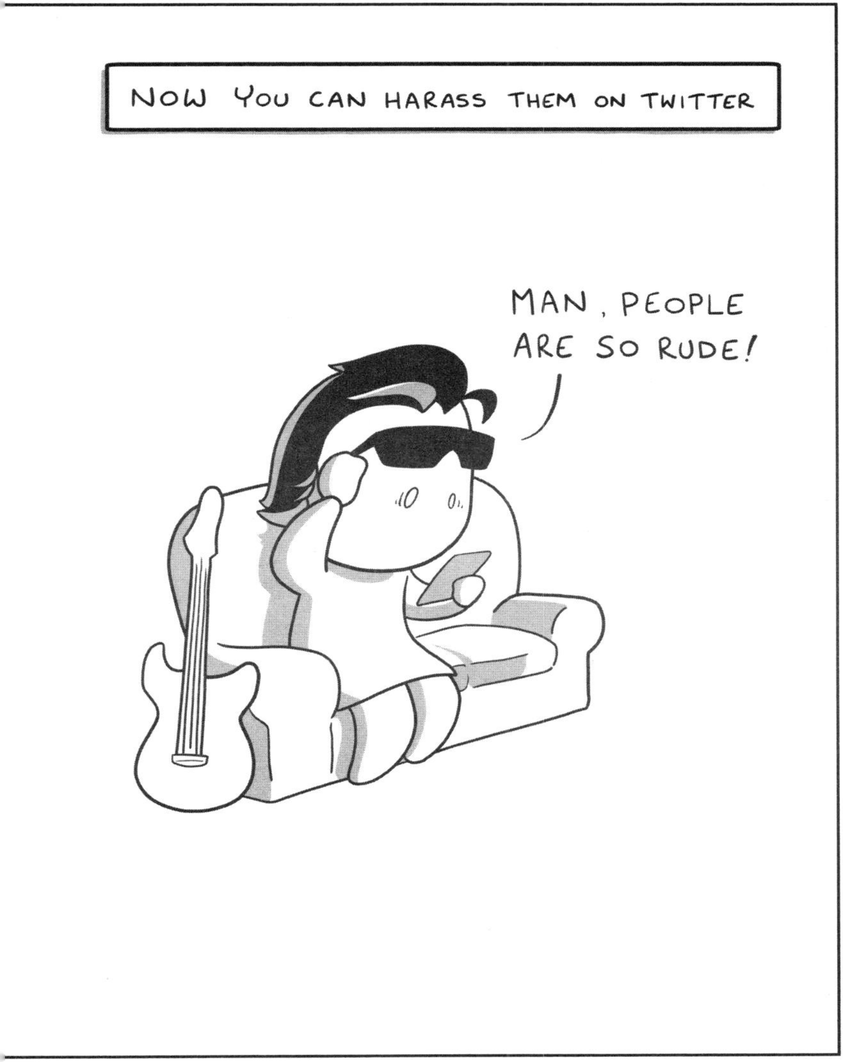
NOW YOU CAN HARASS THEM ON TWITTER
MAN, PEOPLE ARE SO RUDE!

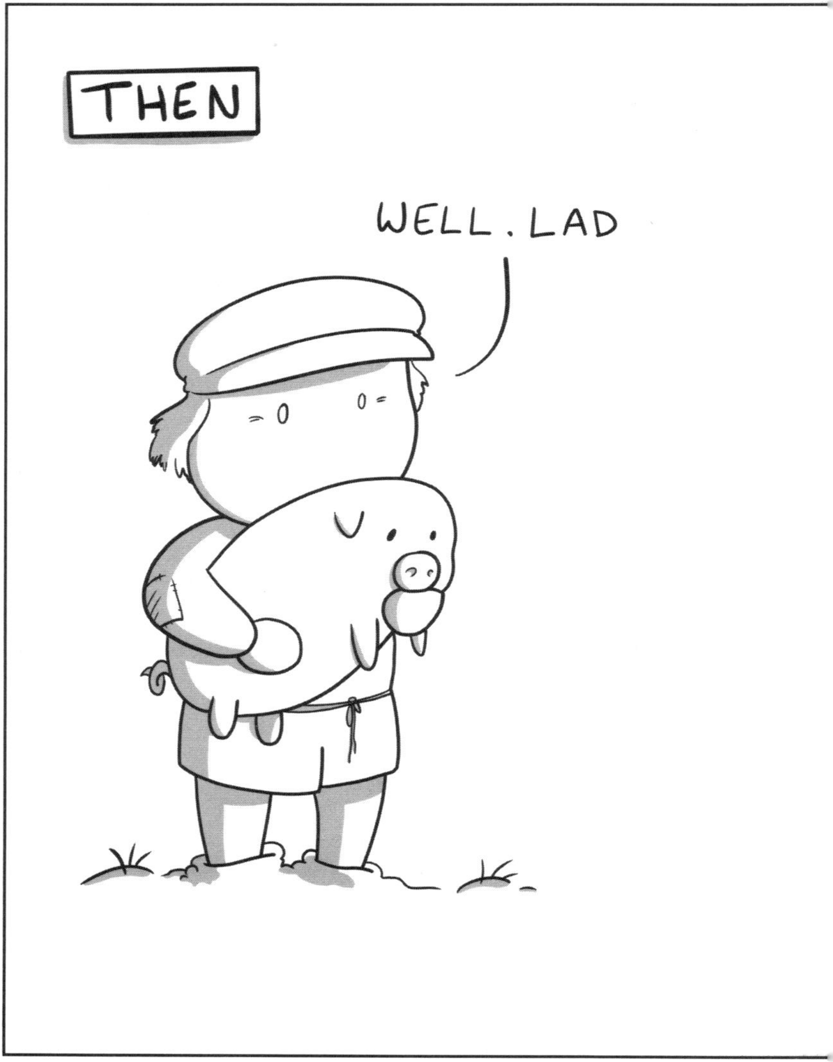
THEN
WELL. LAD

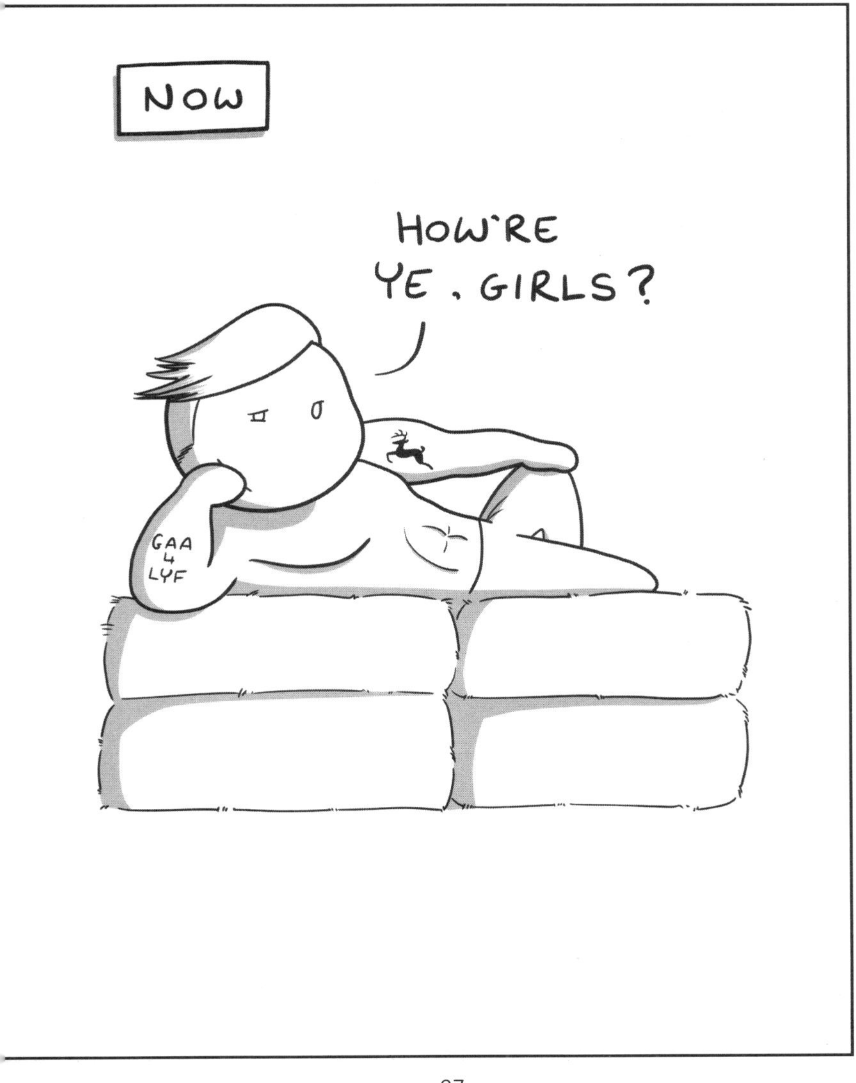
NOW
HOW'RE YE, GIRLS?
GAA 4 LYF

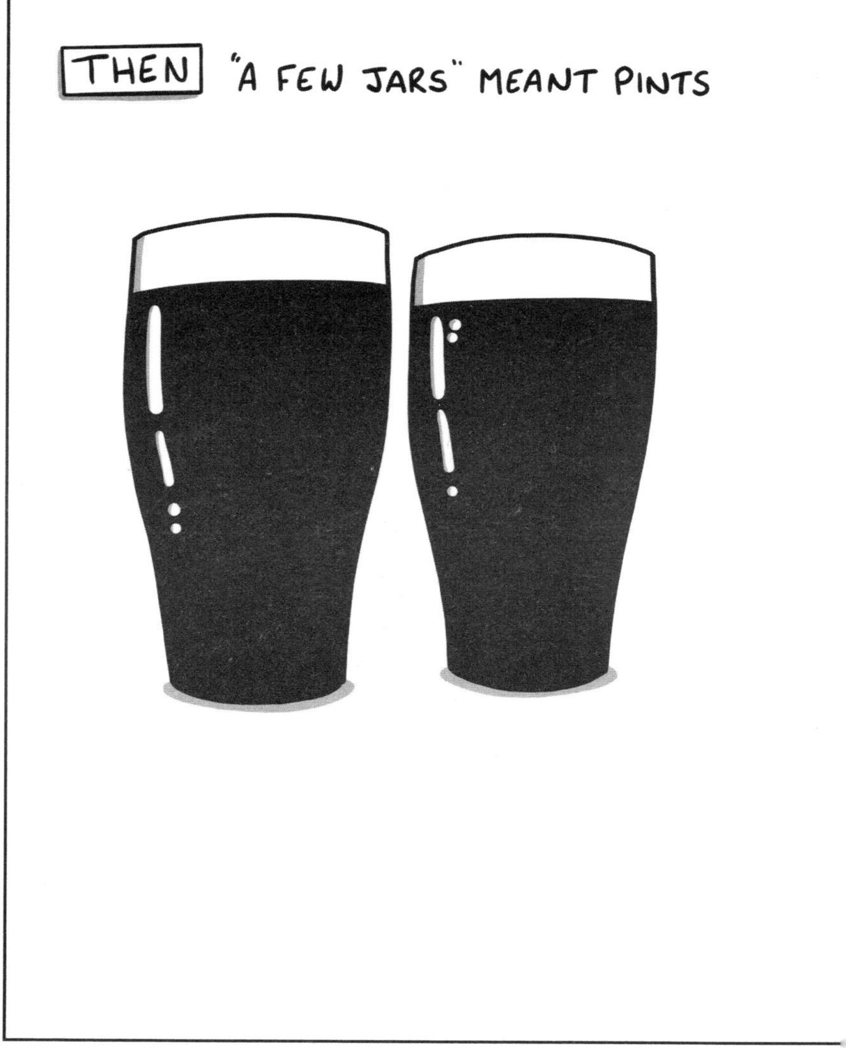
THEN "A FEW JARS" MEANT PINTS

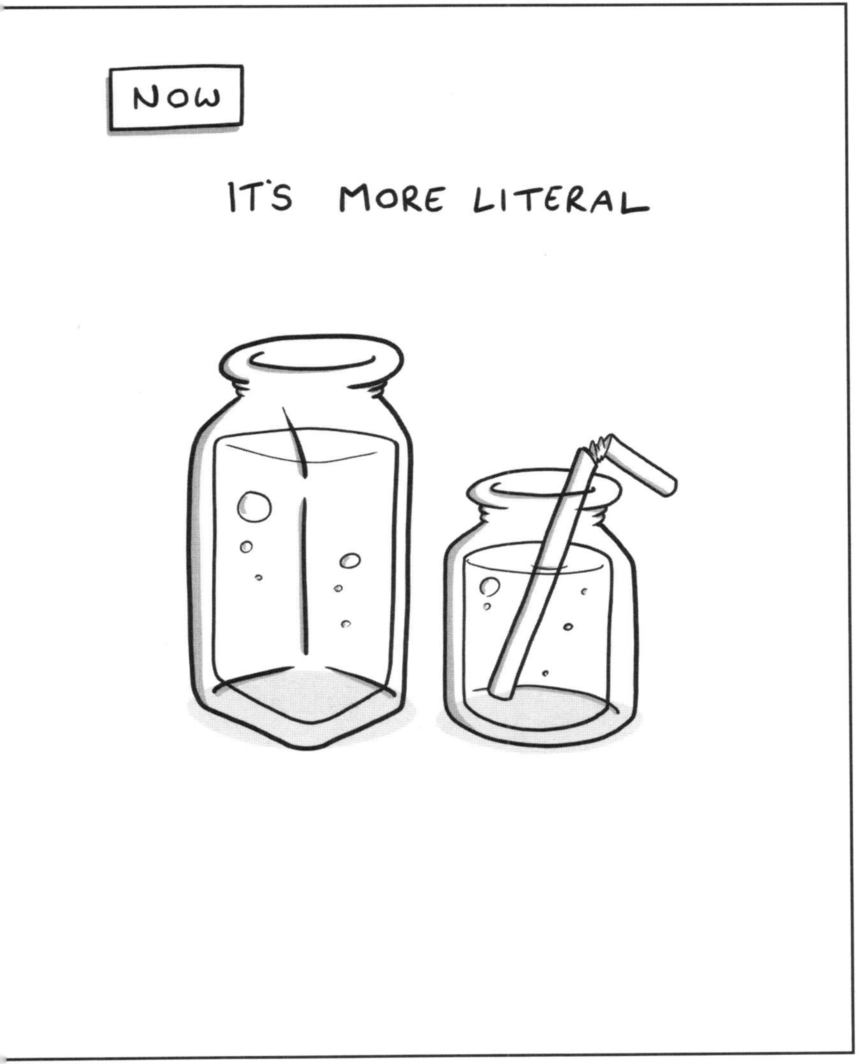
NOW
IT'S MORE LITERAL

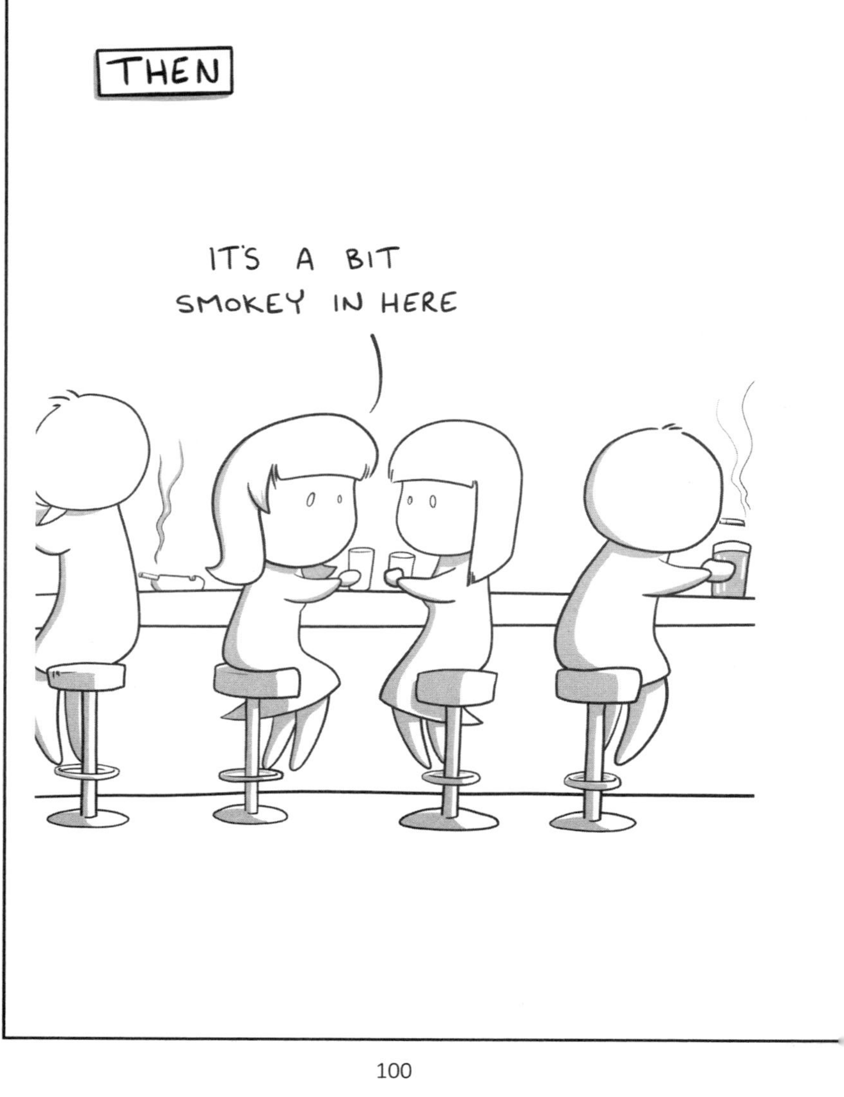
THEN
IT'S A BIT SMOKEY IN HERE

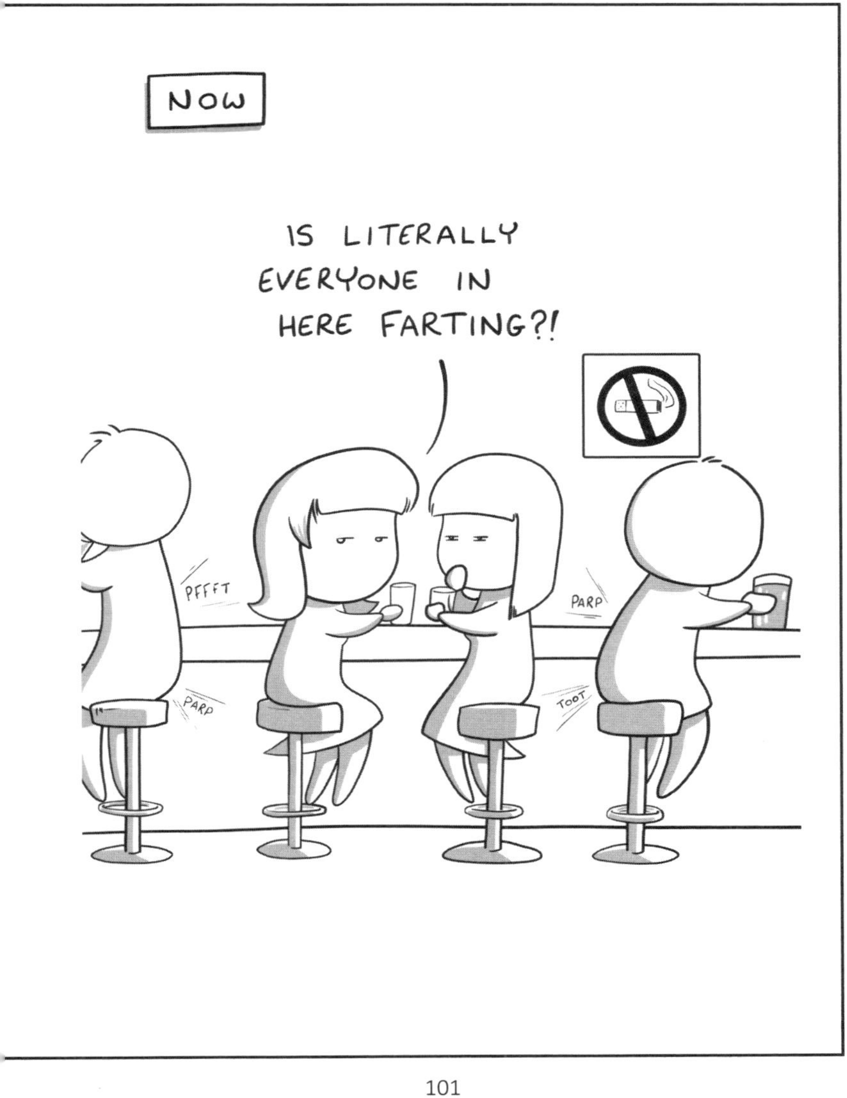
NOW
IS LITERALLY EVERYONE IN HERE FARTING?!
PFFFT
PARP
PARP
TOOT

2B

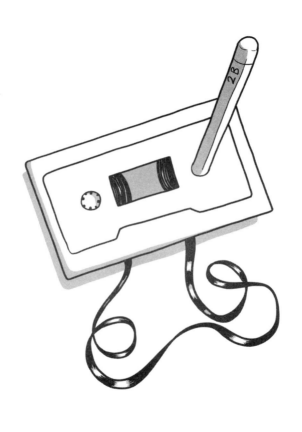

TECHNOLOGY

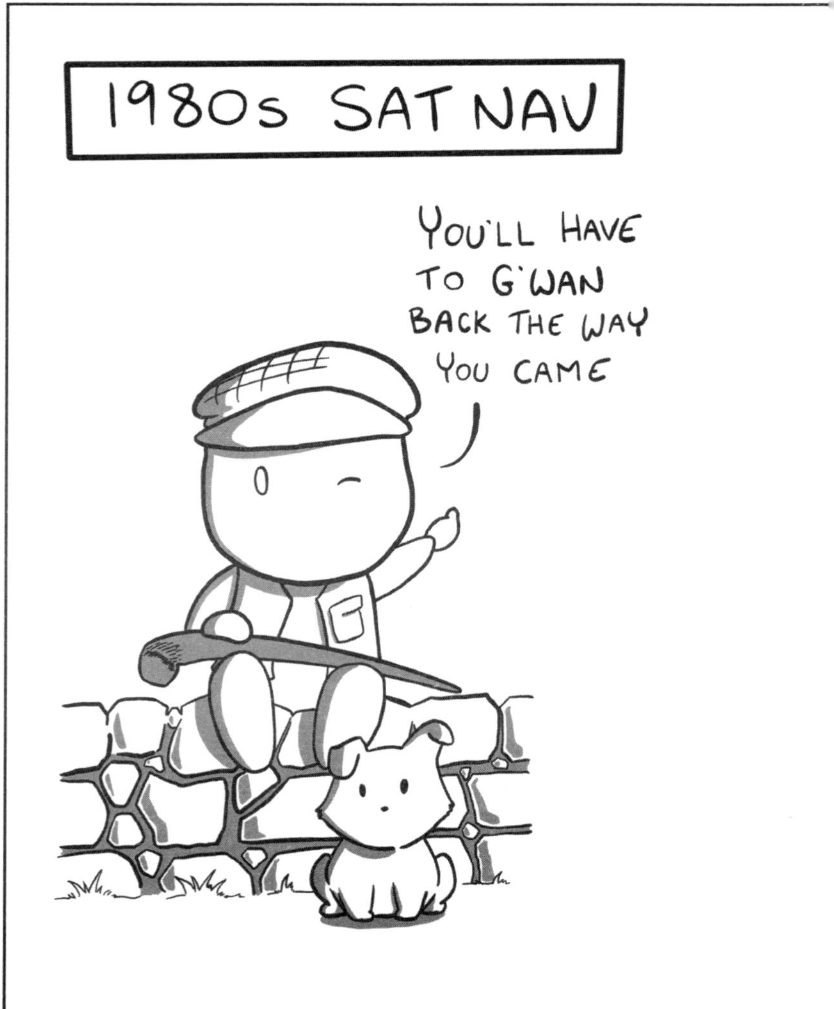
1980s SAT NAV
YOU'LL HAVE TO G'WAN BACK THE WAY YOU CAME

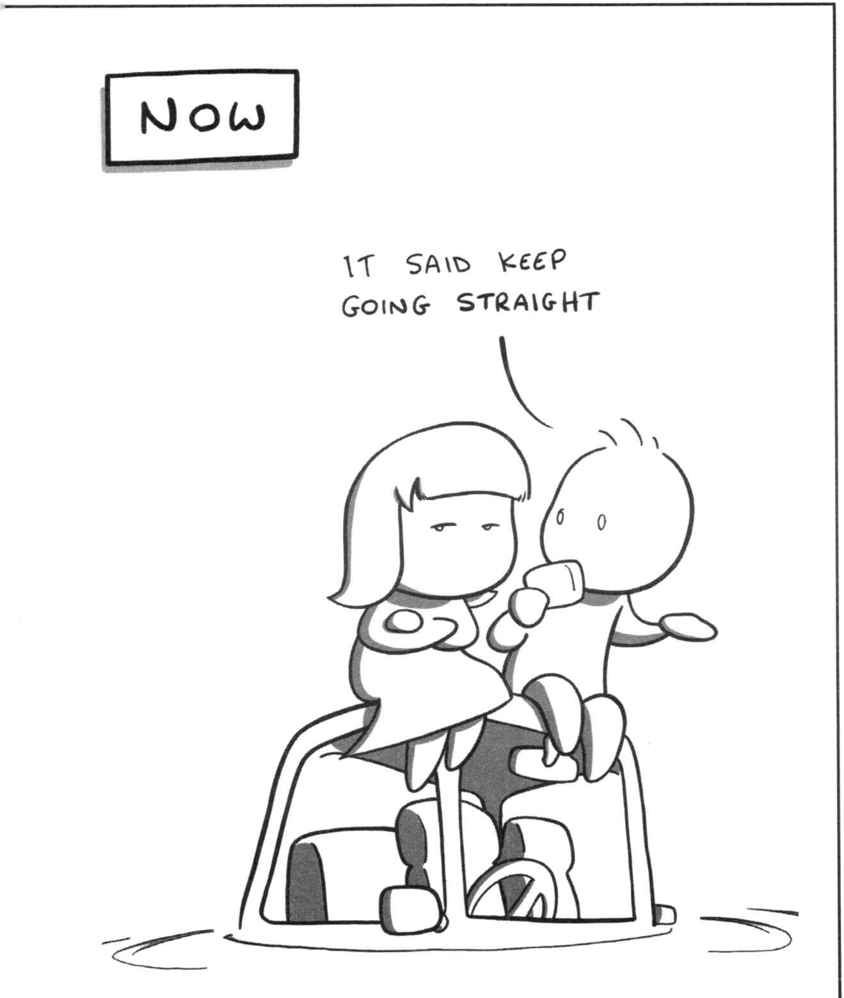
NOW
IT SAID KEEP GOING STRAIGHT

IN THE 80s
YOU NEVER KNEW
WHO WAS CALLING.

NIGHTMARE, RIGHT?

IF YOU WANTED TO
AVOID SOMEONE
YOU'D HAVE A KID
ANSWER FOR YOU.

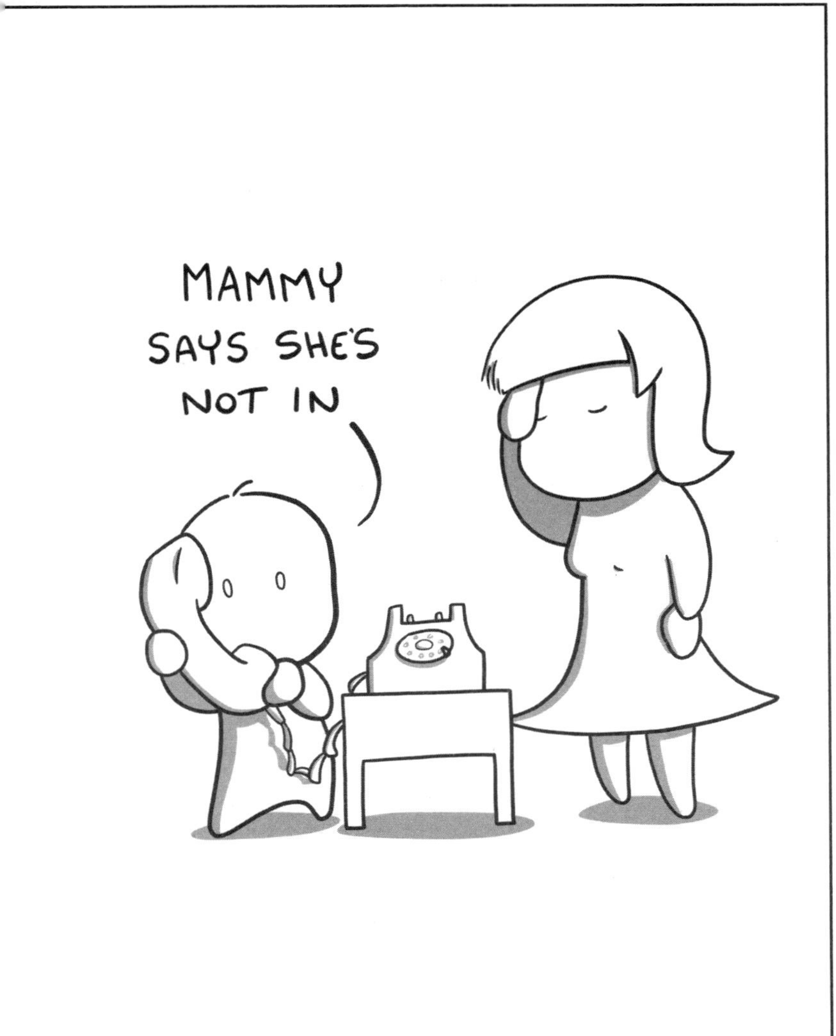
MAMMY SAYS SHE'S NOT IN

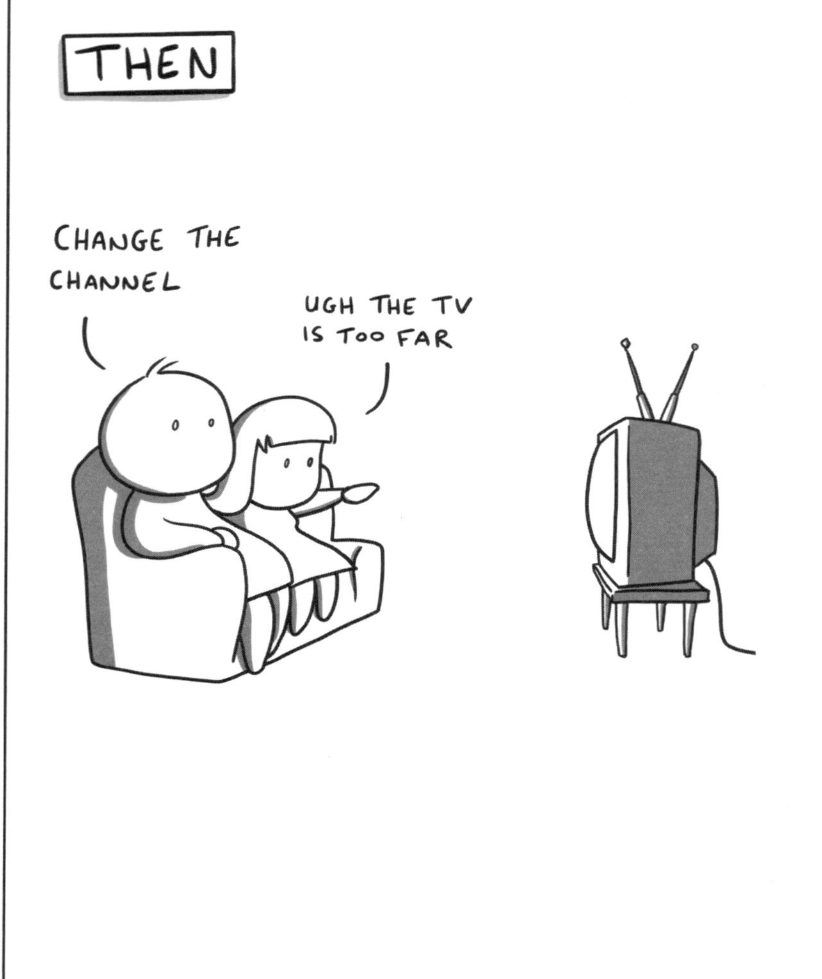
THEN
CHANGE THE CHANNEL
UGH THE TV IS TOO FAR

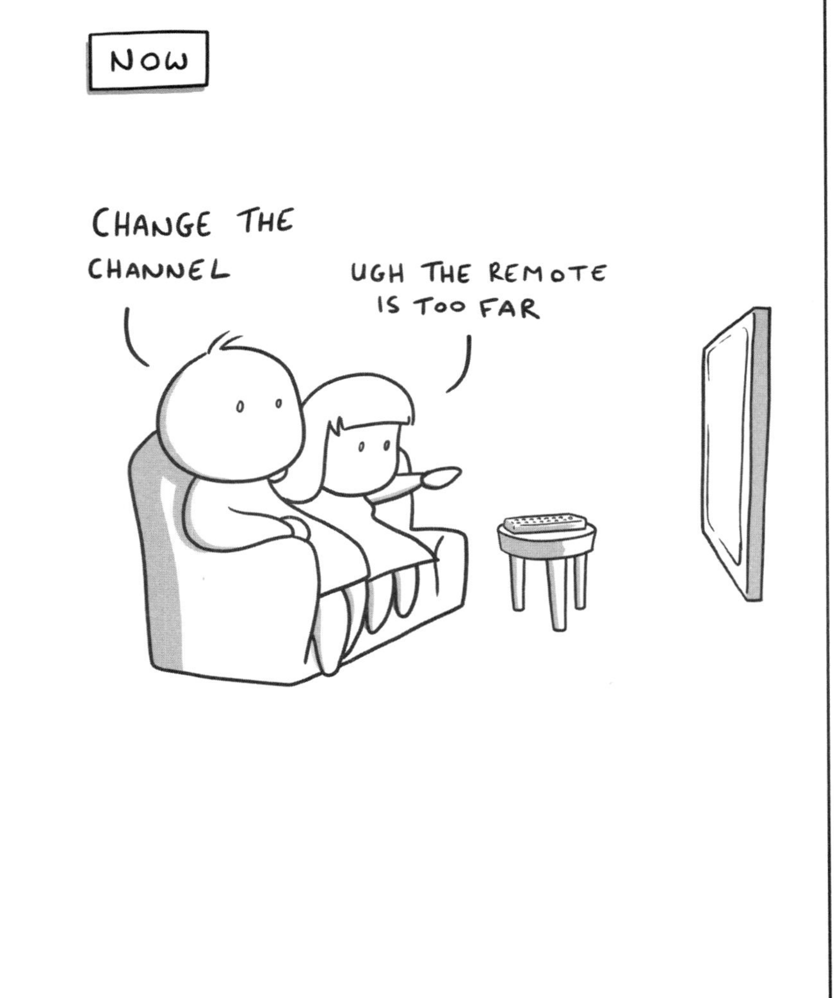
NOW
CHANGE THE CHANNEL
UGH THE REMOTE IS TOO FAR

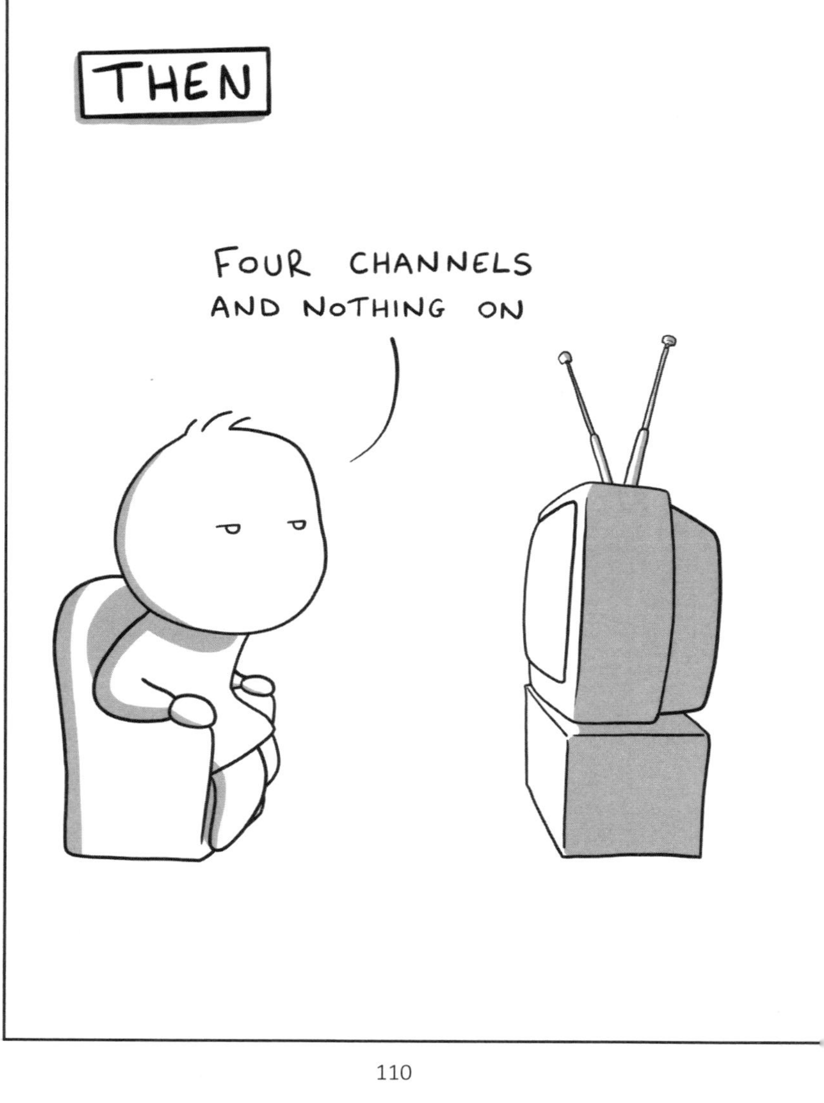
THEN
FOUR CHANNELS AND NOTHING ON

NOW

THREE HUNDRED
CHANNELS AND
NOTHING ON

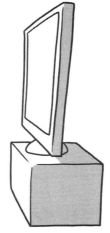

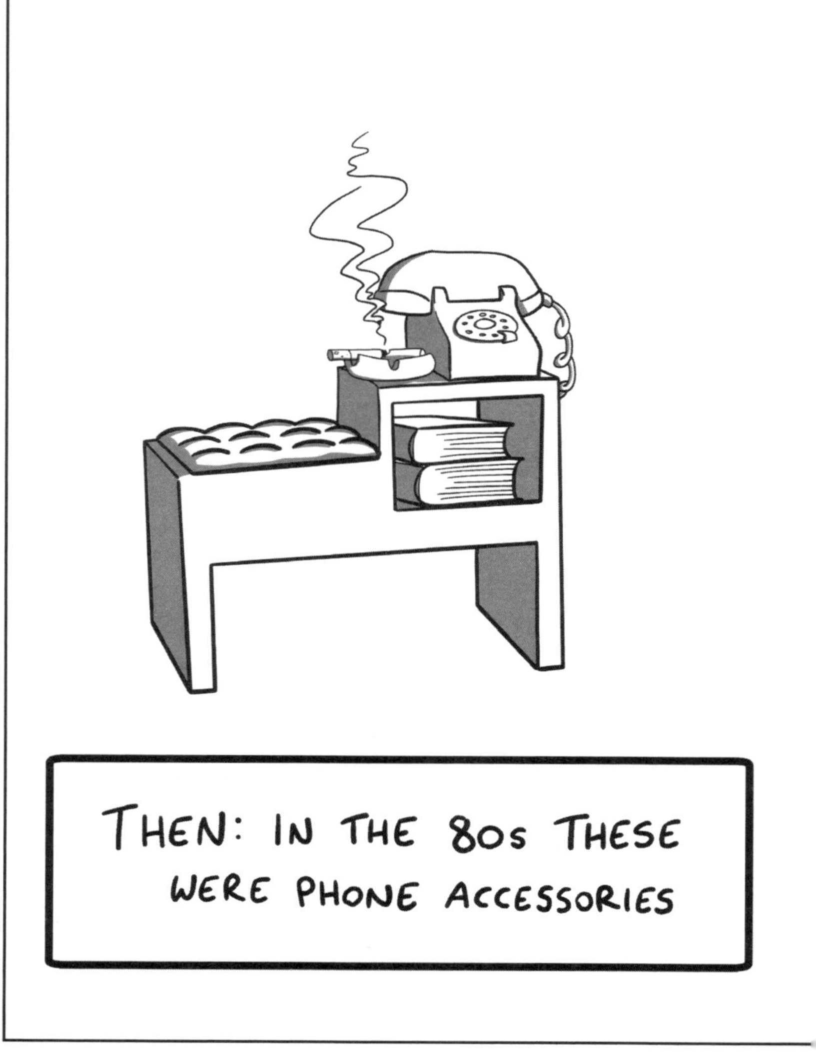
THEN: IN THE 80s THESE WERE PHONE ACCESSORIES

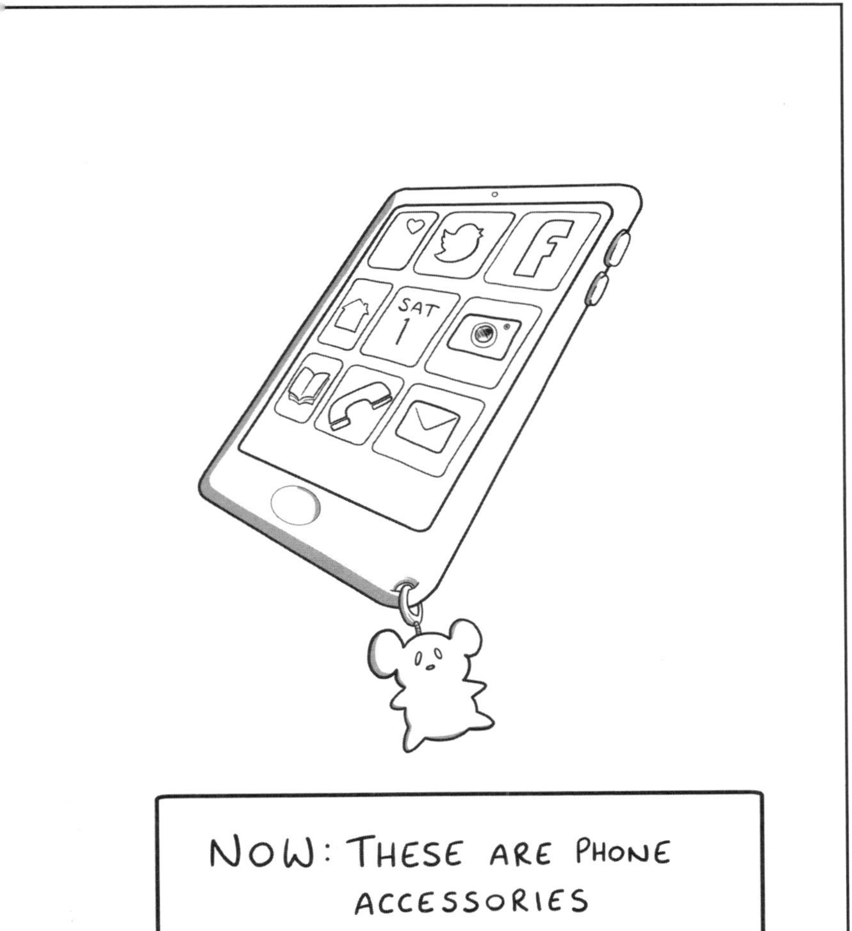
SAT
1
NOW: THESE ARE PHONE ACCESSORIES

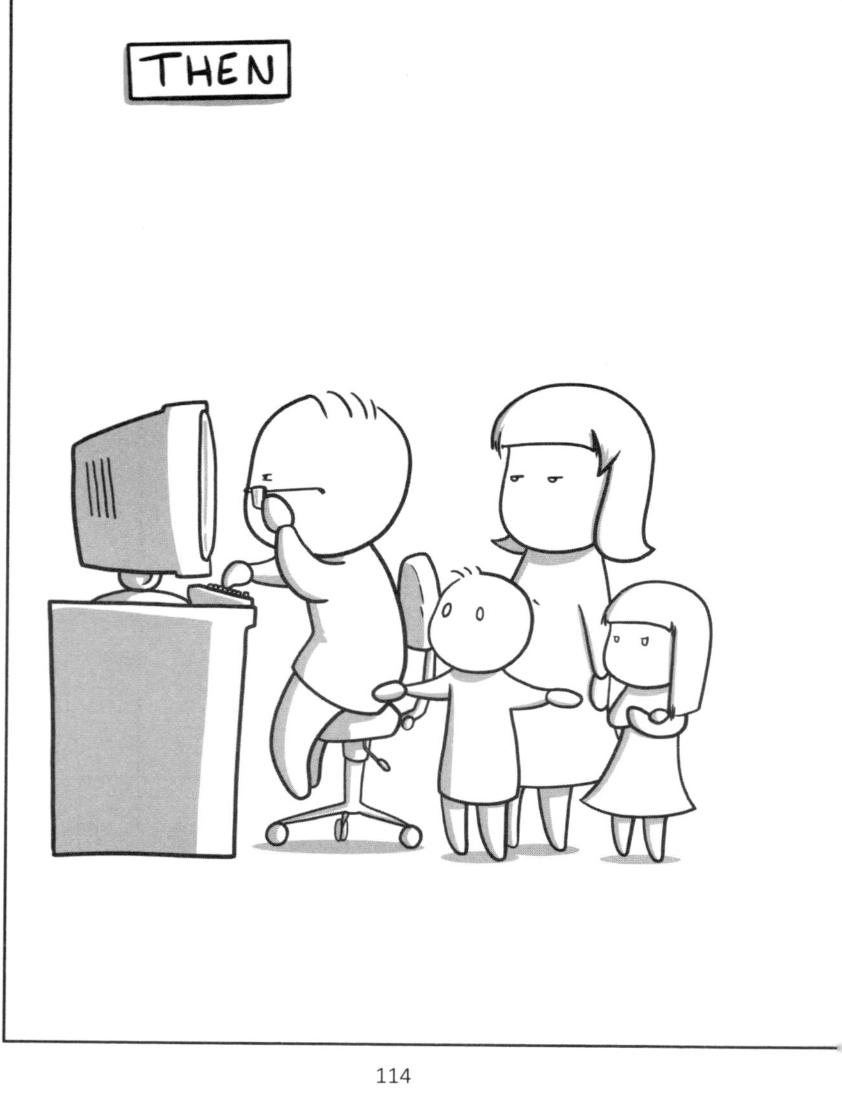
THEN

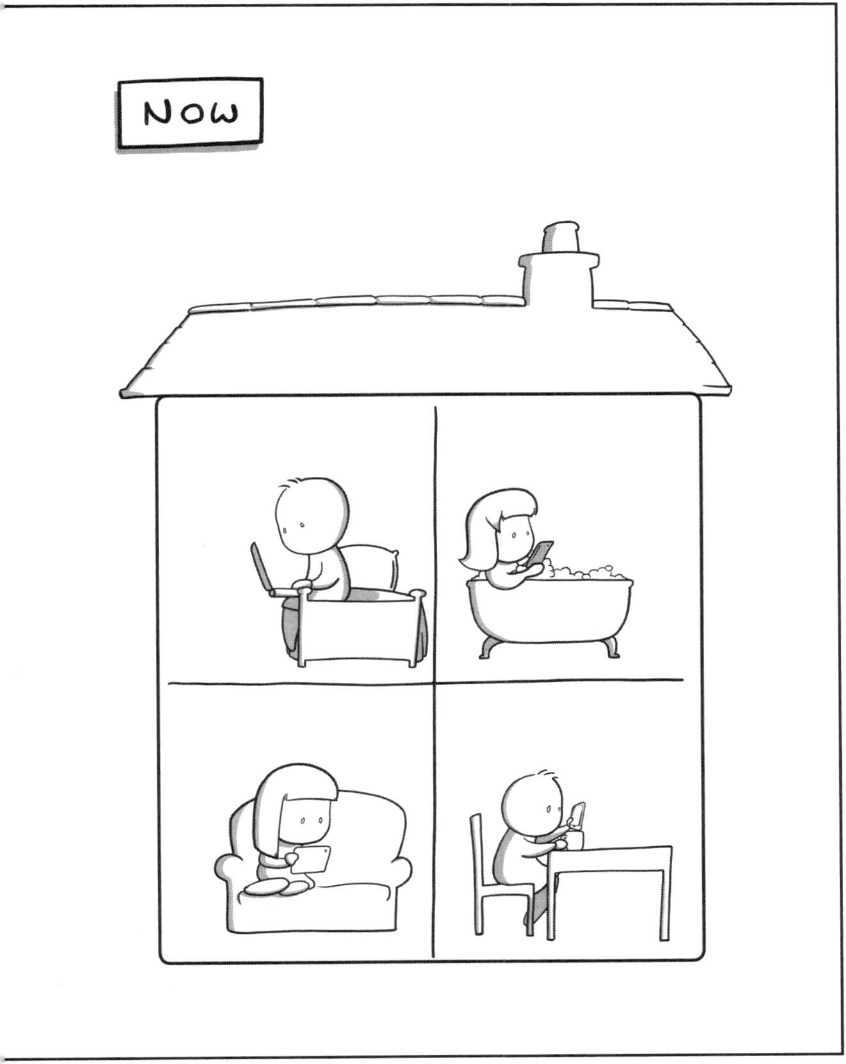
NOW

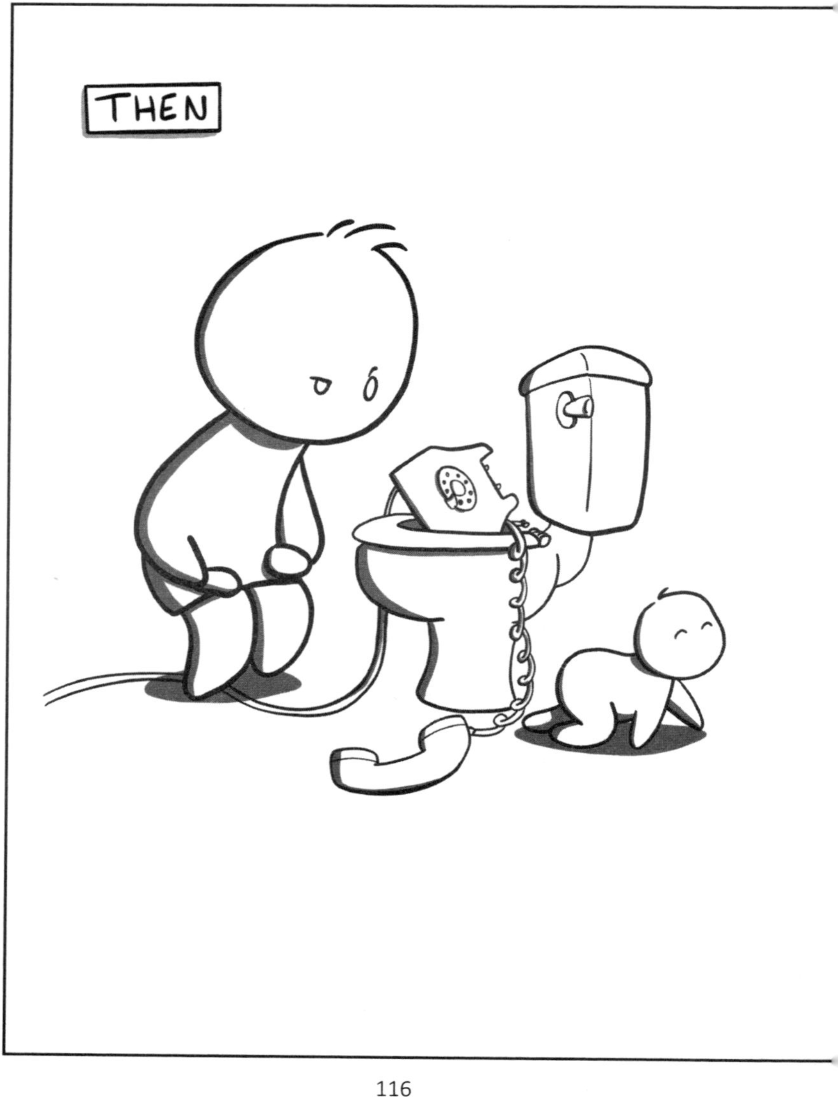
THEN

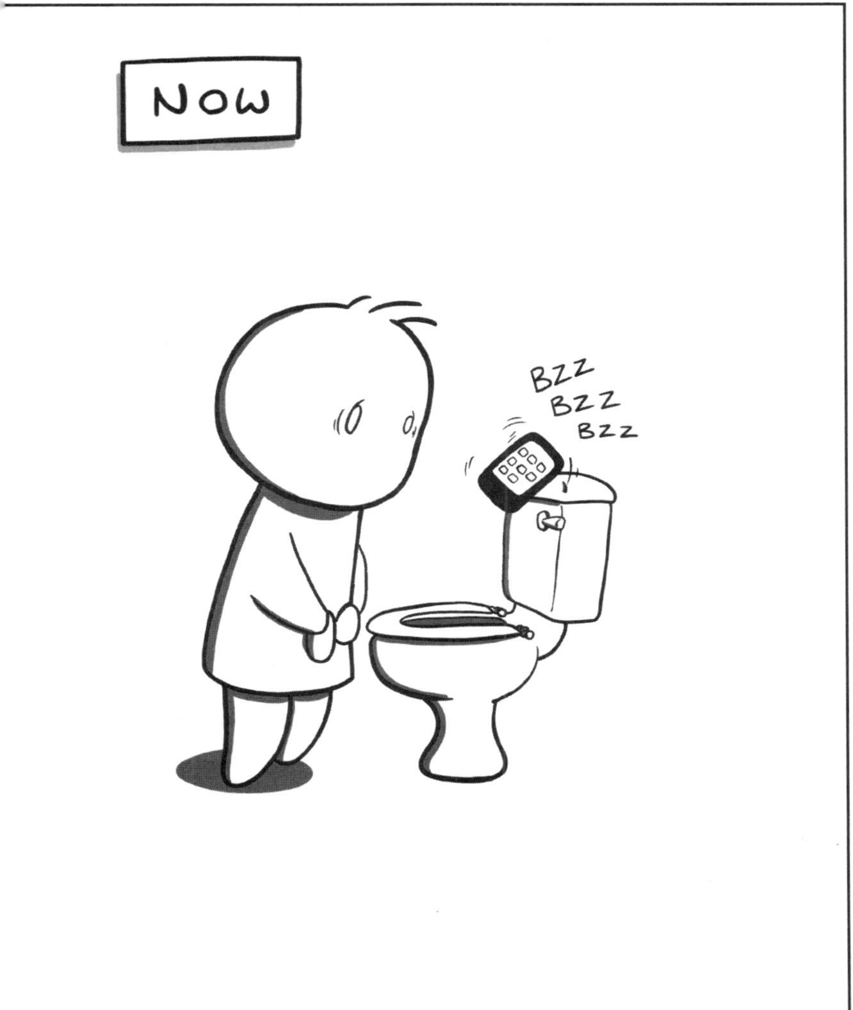
NOW
BZZ
BZZ
BZZ

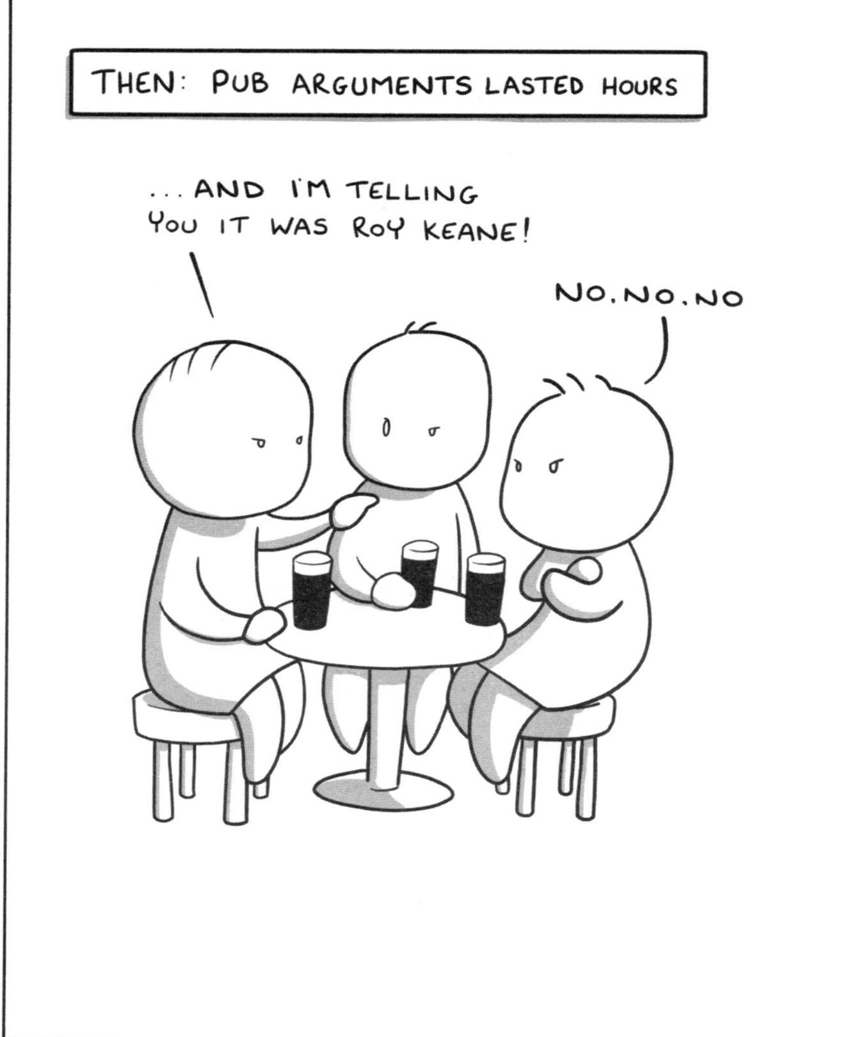
THEN: PUB ARGUMENTS LASTED HOURS
...AND I'M TELLING YOU IT WAS ROY KEANE!
NO.NO.NO

NOW: SMARTPHONES HAVE ENDED THAT
GOOGLED IT. YOU'RE WRONG.
WELL NOW WHAT DO WE ARGUE ABOUT ALL NIGHT?
YEAH!

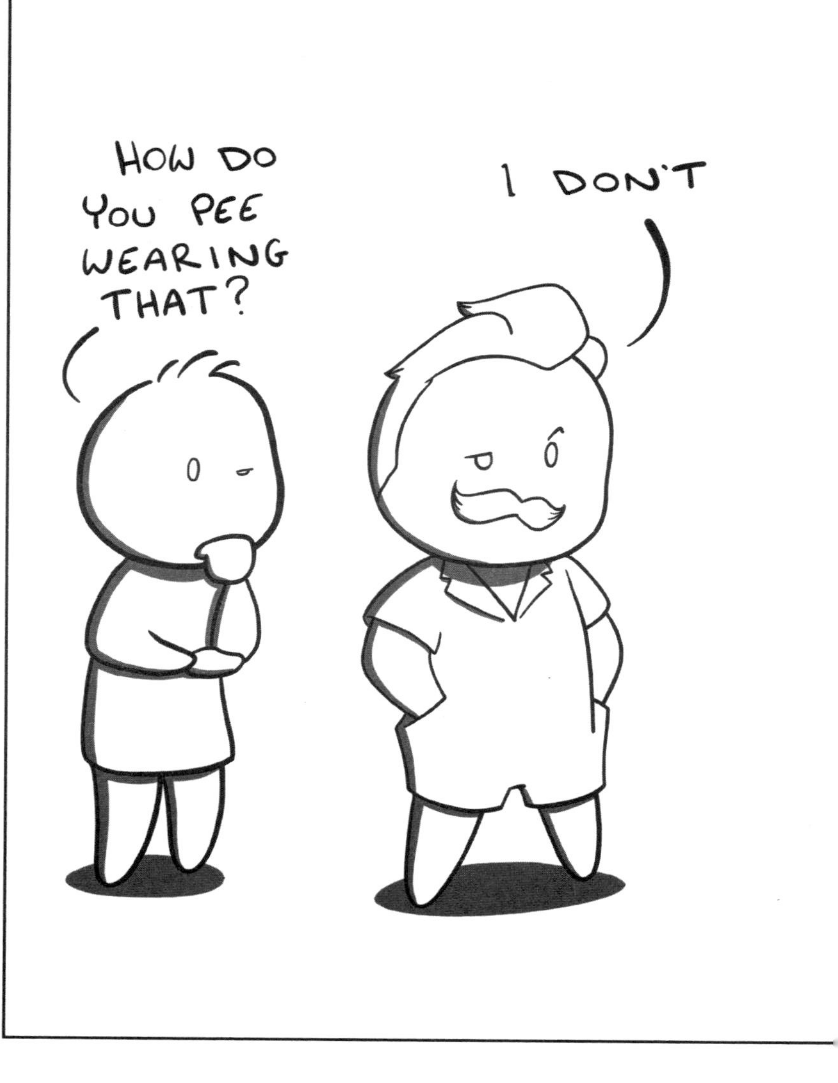
HOW DO YOU PEE WEARING THAT?
I DON'T

TRENDS

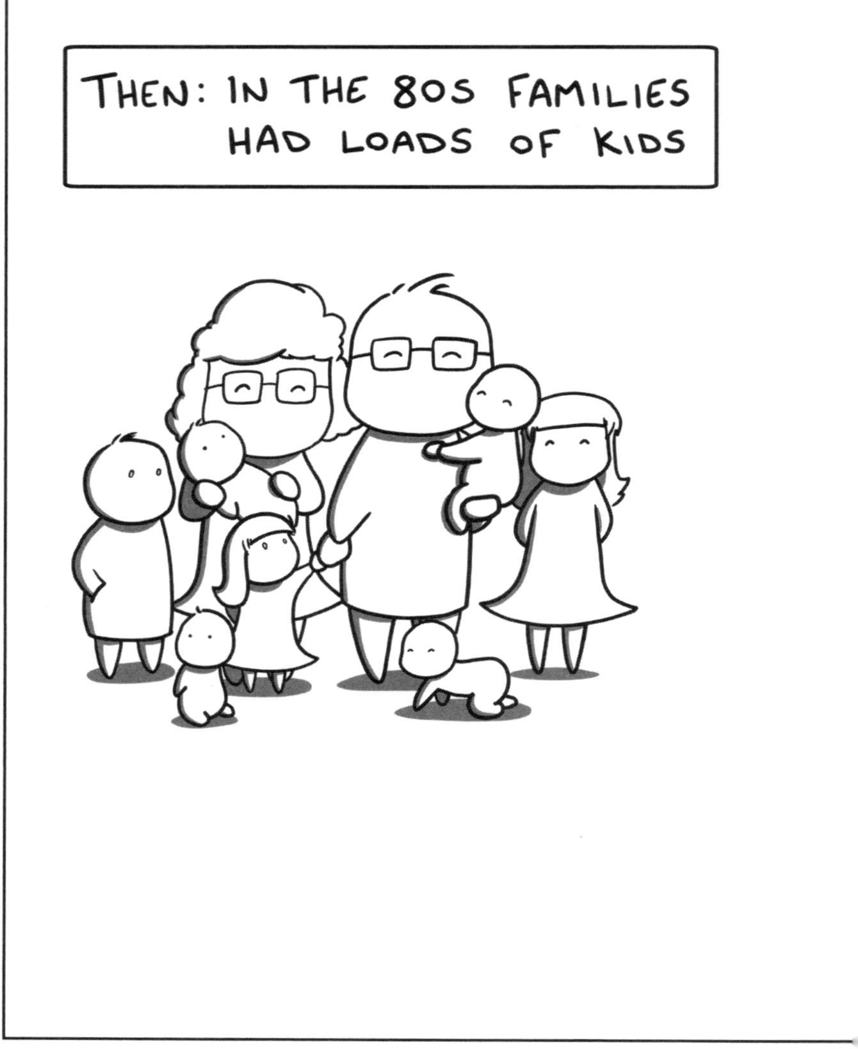
THEN: IN THE 80S FAMILIES HAD LOADS OF KIDS

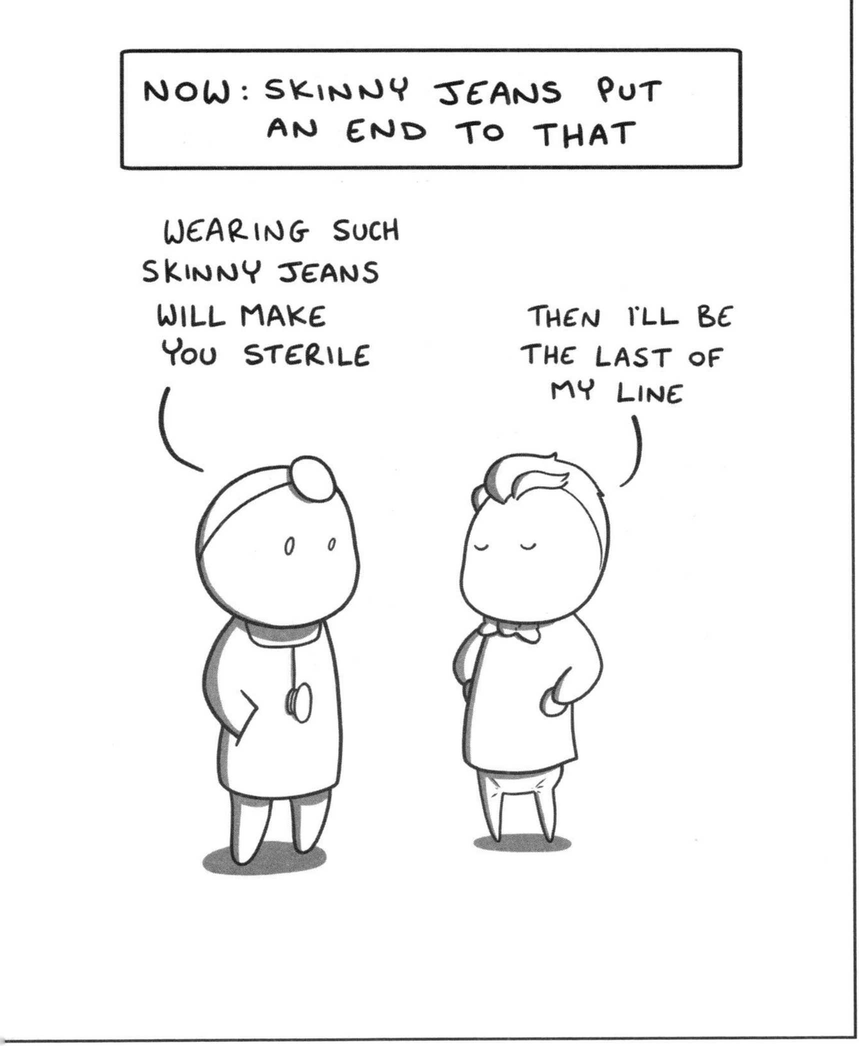
NOW: SKINNY JEANS PUT AN END TO THAT
WEARING SUCH SKINNY JEANS WILL MAKE YOU STERILE
THEN I'LL BE THE LAST OF MY LINE

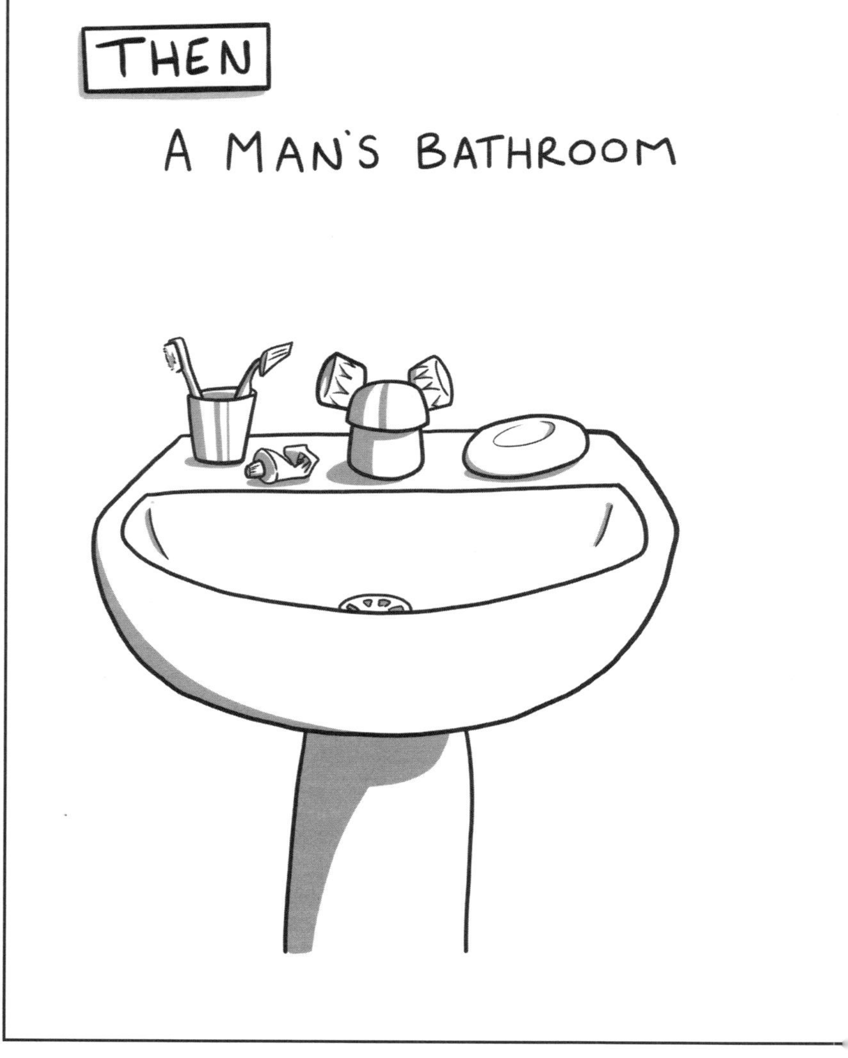
THEN
A MAN'S BATHROOM

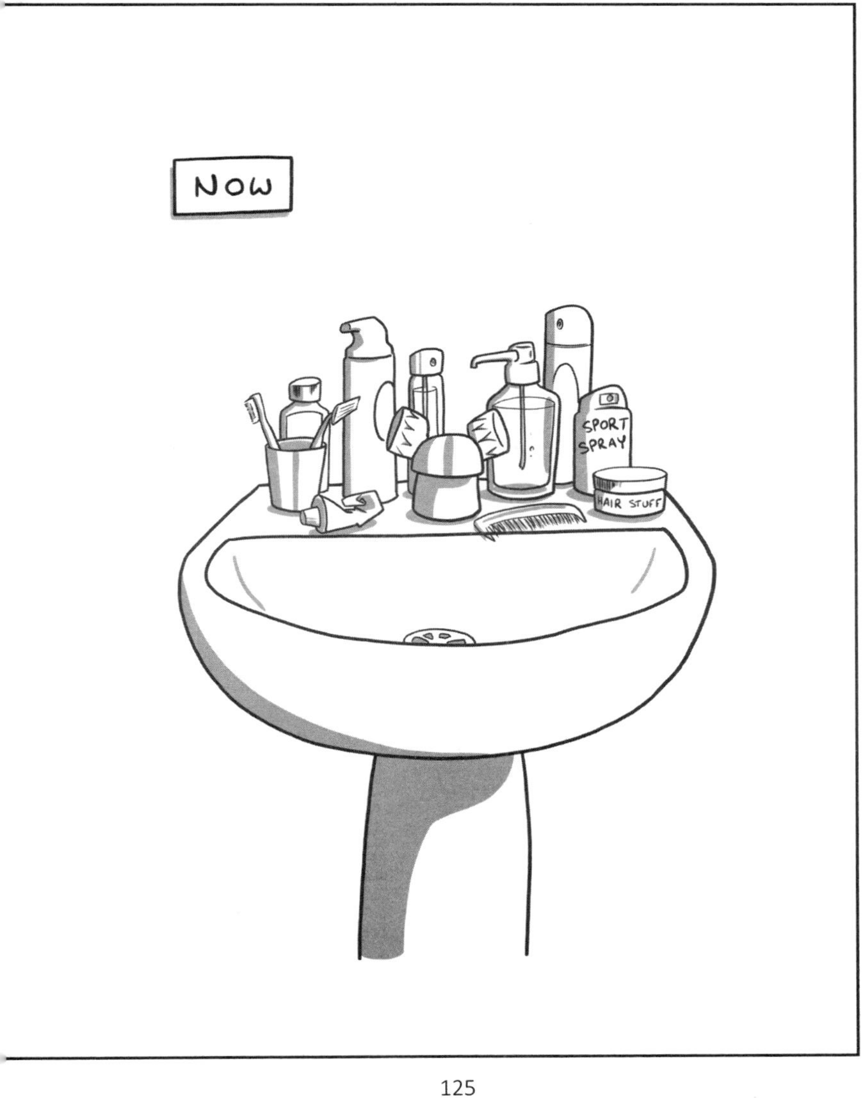
NOW
SPORT SPRAY
HAIR STUFF

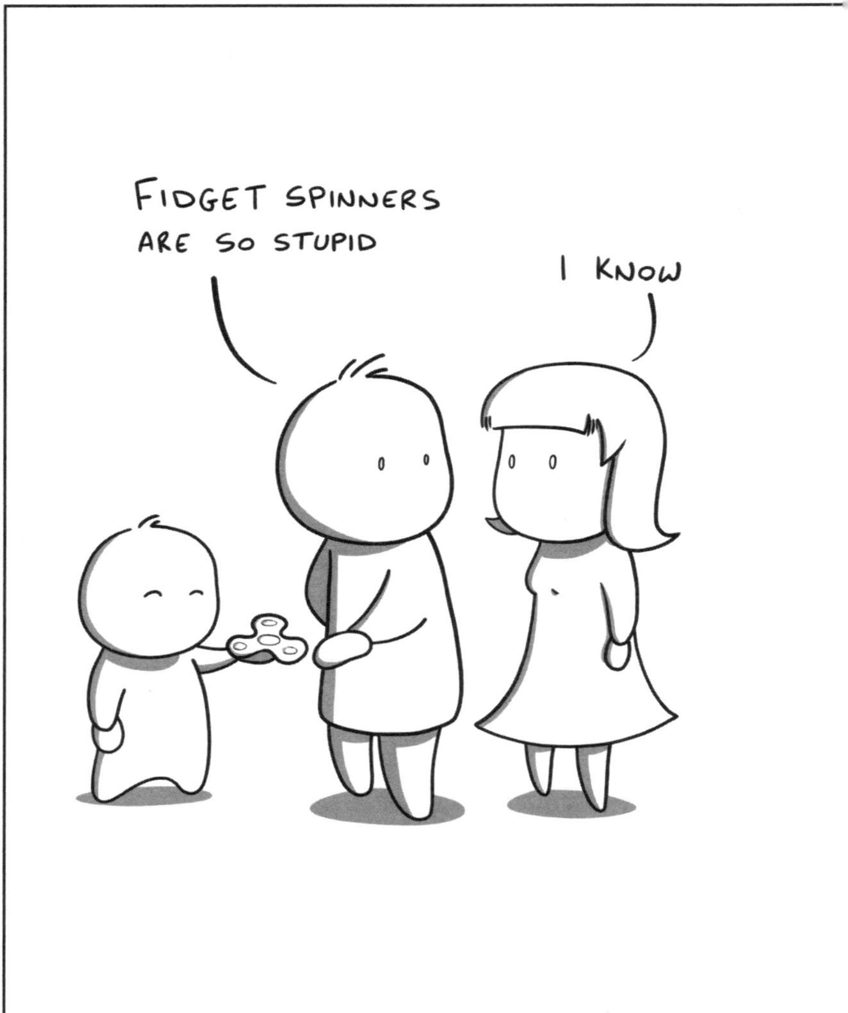
FIDGET SPINNERS ARE SO STUPID
I KNOW

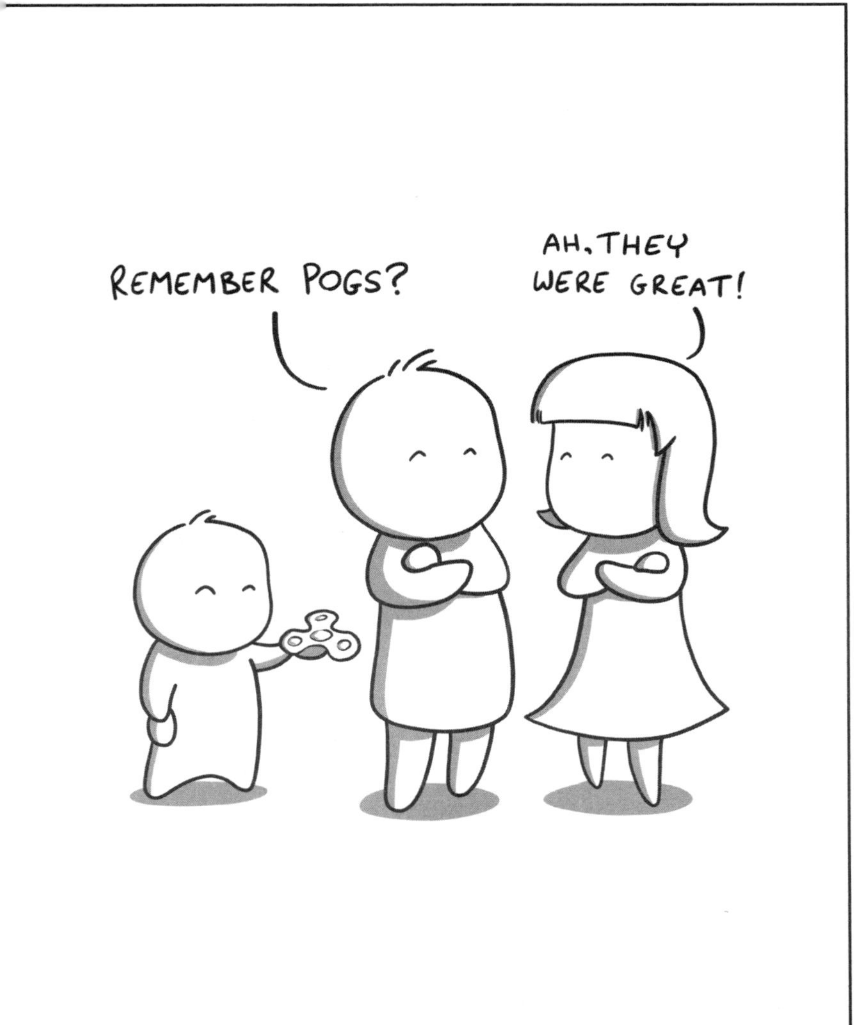
REMEMBER POGS?
AH, THEY WERE GREAT!

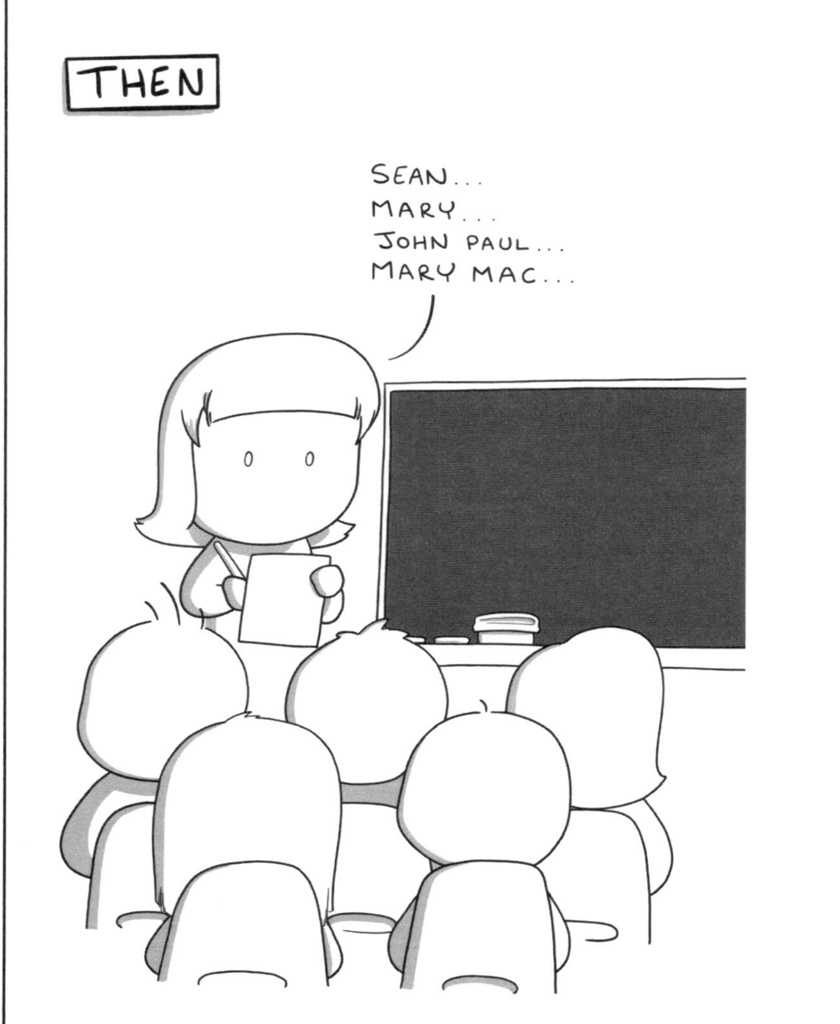
THEN
SEAN...
MARY...
JOHN PAUL...
MARY MAC...

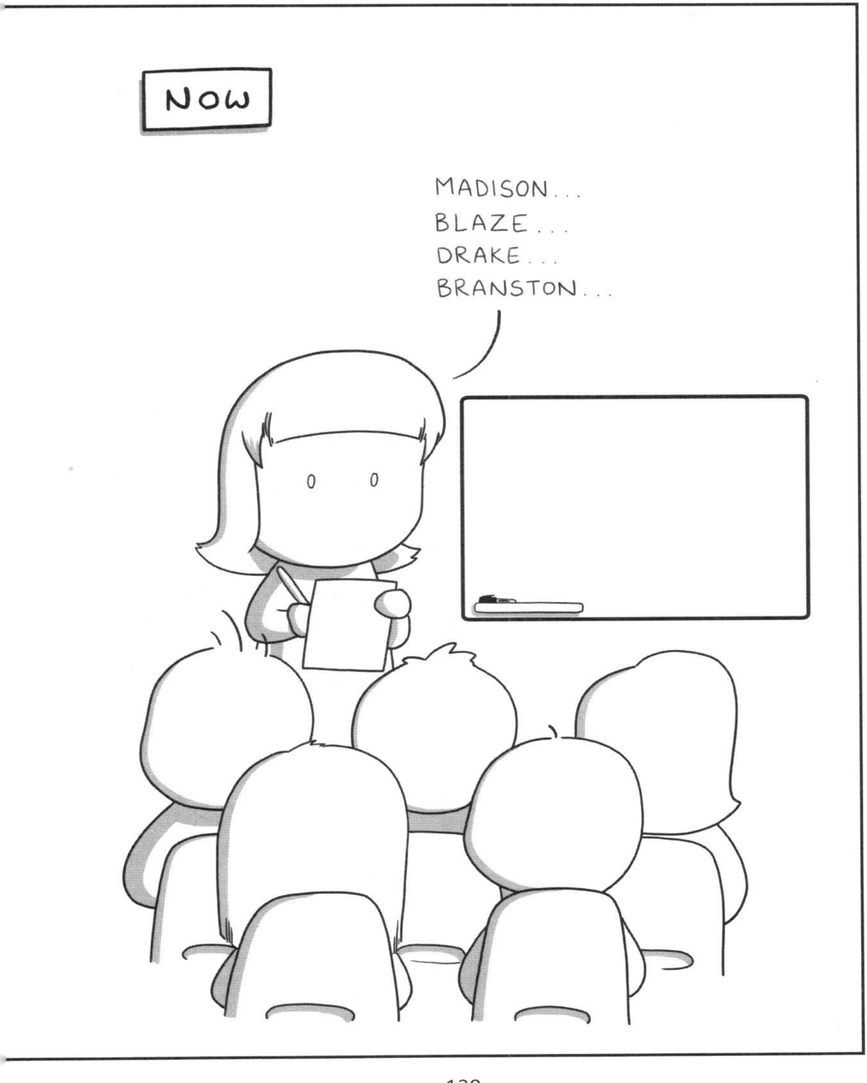
NOW
MADISON...
BLAZE...
DRAKE...
BRANSTON...

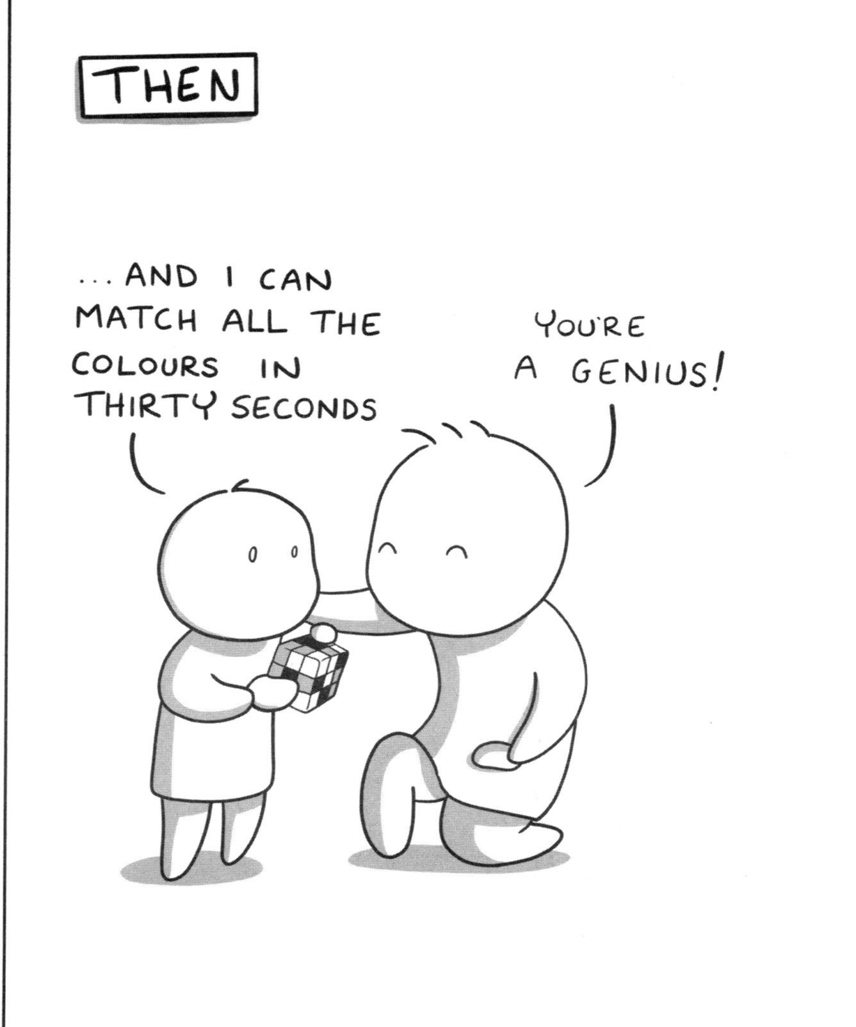
THEN
...AND I CAN MATCH ALL THE COLOURS IN THIRTY SECONDS
YOU'RE A GENIUS!

NOW
...AND I FLIP THE BOTTLE UNTIL T LANDS LIKE THIS
WE'RE GETTING YOU A TUTOR

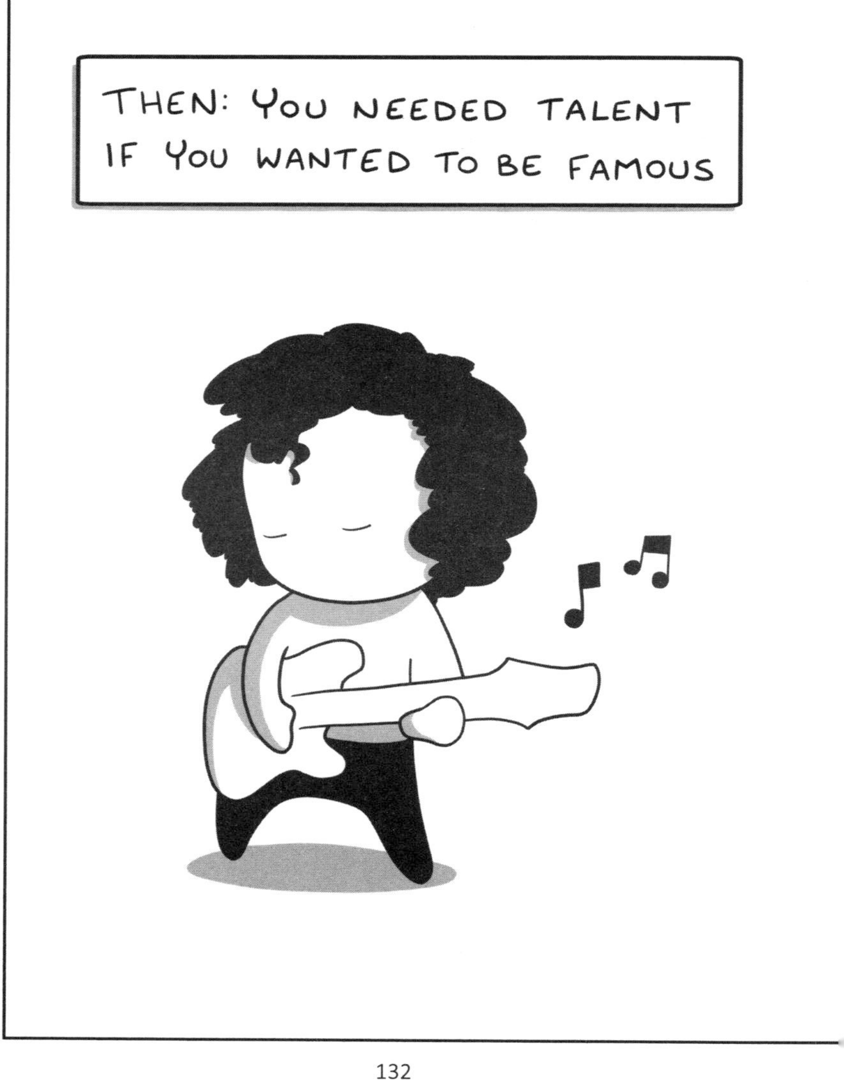
THEN: YOU NEEDED TALENT IF YOU WANTED TO BE FAMOUS

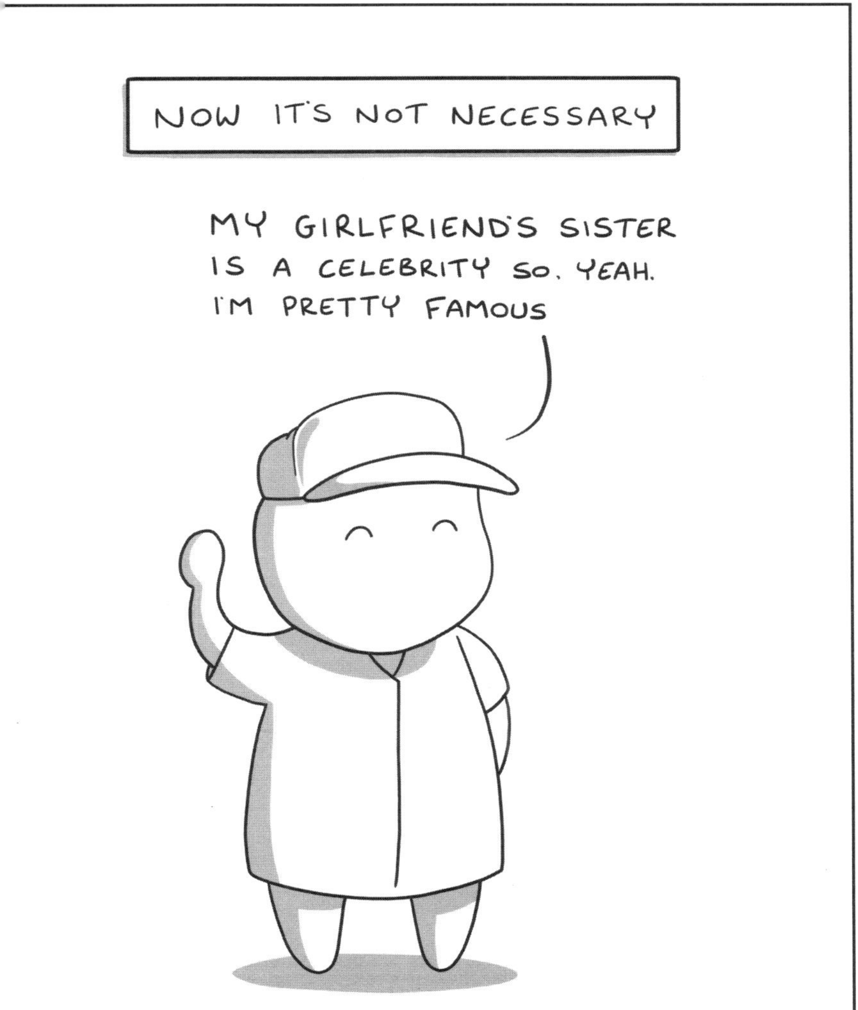
NOW IT'S NOT NECESSARY
MY GIRLFRIEND'S SISTER IS A CELEBRITY SO. YEAH. I'M PRETTY FAMOUS

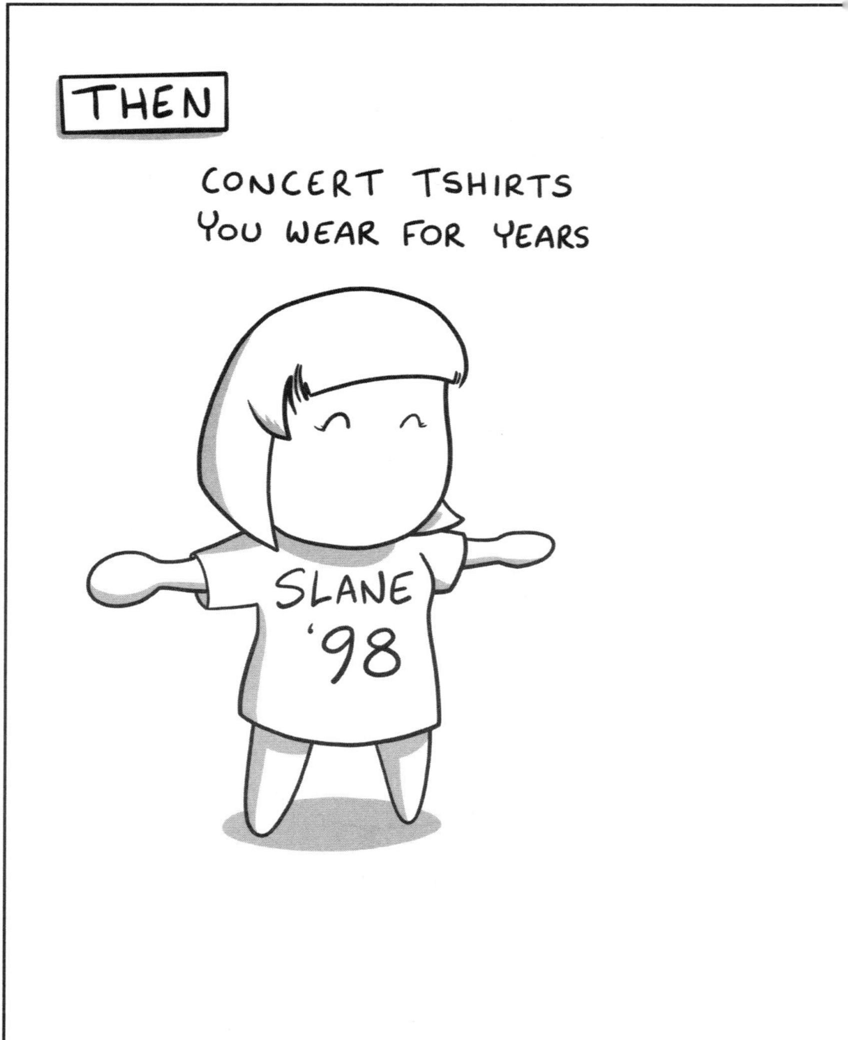
THEN
CONCERT TSHIRTS
YOU WEAR FOR YEARS
SLANE
'98

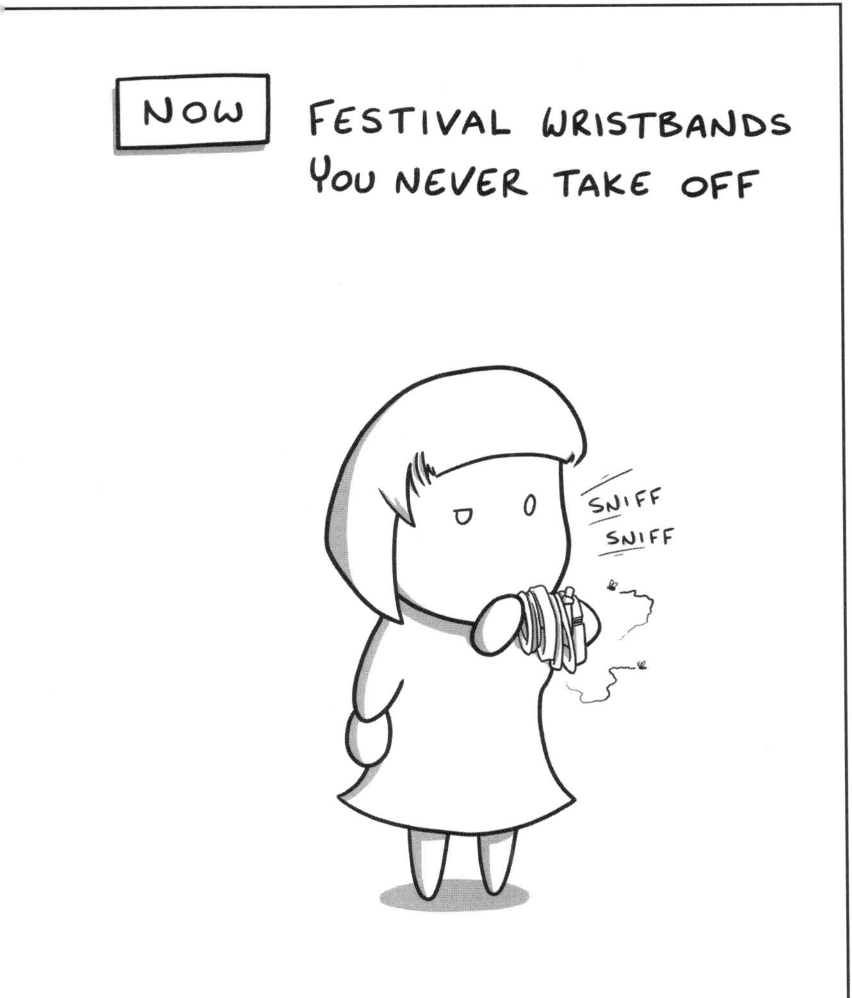
NOW
FESTIVAL WRISTBANDS YOU NEVER TAKE OFF
SNIFF
SNIFF

ACKNOWLEDGEMENTS

HUGE THANKS TO EVERYONE IN HACHETTE ESPECIALLY CIARA CONSIDINE FOR HER INPUT IN GETTING THE BOOK FINISHED.